FRIENDS
OF ACPL

INDONESIAN FLAVORS

D1551825

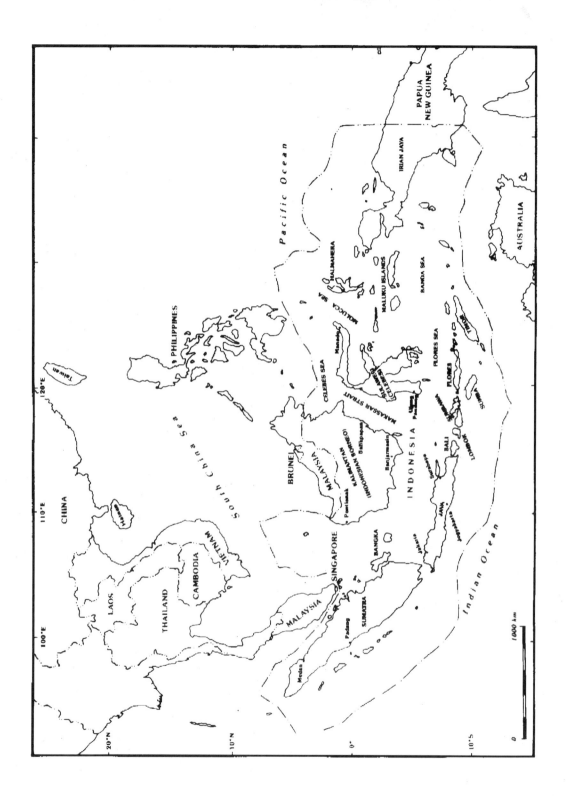

INDONESIAN FLAVORS

SUSAN ANDERSON

FROG, LTD.
BERKELEY, CALIFORNIA

INDONESIAN FLAVORS

Published by Frog, Ltd.

Frog, Ltd. books are distributed by
North Atlantic Books
P.O. Box 12327
Berkeley, California 94712

Cover and interior (pp. vii–40) photography by Susan Anderson
Printed in the United States of America

Library of Congress Cataloging-in-Publication Data
Anderson, Susan.
    Indonesian Flavors/Susan Anderson.
        p. cm.
    Includes bibliographical references and index.
    ISBN 1-883319-28-5 (trade paper)
    1. Cookery, Indonesian. 2. Food habits—Indonesia. I. Title.
    TX724.5.I5A84 1995
    95-18916   CIP

1 2 3 4 5 6 7 8 9 / 99 98 97 96 95

CONTENTS

ACKNOWLEDGMENTS

I would like to thank the following people for allowing me access to their restaurants in Jakarta and to photograph their premises and dishes: Bpk Oom Mucharam, General Manager, and Ibu Malia Soenario, at the Oasis Restaurant; Bpk Soekardi, Operations Manager, at the Raden Kuring Restaurant; Bpk P. Mendhung, Assistant Manager at the Nyonya Suharti Rumah Makan; Bpk Purwadi at the Sari Kuring Restaurant; Bpk H. Anwar at the Sari Bundo Padang Restaurant; and Nyonya Lani at the Along Restaurant.

I would also like to thank Bpk Tedi Kresna Wardhana for his photography, as well as my husband, Ian, for all his encouragement in the compilation of these recipes.

FOREWORD

Indonesia's tropical sun, sea, and very rich soil have provided the ingredients to shape a cuisine which could be described as something between Indian and Chinese food. Indonesian dishes have been influenced by various invaders and settlers over the centuries, and they encompass all, from the everyday to the very special.

Indonesian cooking is essentially of the village. The combination of contrasting flavors, textures, and colors distinguishes the cuisine and unifies the various regional styles. No hard and fast culinary rules have ever been laid down in this method of cooking. Many of the following recipes are traditional, but many are simply the results of experiments with well known dishes. Restaurants in Indonesia are rather unromantically called *rumah makan*, literally meaning "house of eating."

Several dishes are usually present at one meal, which is not that daunting for the cook because food is often served at room temperature. Everything is generally served together: soups, side dishes, sauces, meats, fish,

The cooking smells from street stalls leave a lingering impression on the visitor to Indonesia.

vegetables, fruits, etc. Alcohol is not usually consumed; instead sweet tea and black *kopi tubruk* (a very strong and "earthy" drink) and fresh fruit or coconut juice are served with a meal. Indonesian meals are always leisurely, communal, and hospitable affairs.

Indonesian cuisine can be very refreshing. From the poorest road stall to the most fashionable restaurant, something can be discovered. This book is a collection of the many flavors to be found and enjoyed in Indonesia.

(Above): Often many members from one family will staff one stand. (Right): Pungent aromas mark the spice vendor's stall.

INDONESIAN FLAVORS

INTRODUCTION

The History, Food, and Customs of the Indonesian Archipelago

Indonesia—a country of 13,000 islands—lies at the crossroads of the ancient East-West trade routes, where many sophisticated early civilizations flourished from very early times. Indeed, one of the first indications of man's presence on earth was found on Java: "Java Man" is a skull which is thought to date from a quarter- to a half-million years ago.

Indonesia's islands are strung along the equator and over 6,000 of them are inhabited. If people are aware of Indonesia at all they probably tend to think of the five largest islands of Java, Sumatra, Borneo (Kalimantan), Sulawesi, and Irian Jaya; and of course the popular holiday destinations of Bali and Lombok.

With a population of over 180 million, Indonesia is the fourth most populous country in the world. A large percentage of the population is extremely poor and, until very recently, large families were the norm, to provide a type of insurance policy for senior members in old age and through illness.

The marketplace is always a potpourri of color and aroma. Next page, fishermen leaving the harbor.

Indonesians have always believed very strongly in the forces of nature; spirits must be appeased, and the idea of magic has great force. Even though much of the younger generation is now drawn to Western habits, the old animism is still widespread. A *selamatan,* or a rite seeking favors of the spirits, is still carried out when something as basic as a new house is completed, and witch doctors *(dukuns)* are consulted to exorcise evil.

Indonesia's history is full of stories of invaders, settlers, and the influence of the major religions and cultures of the world. Its main historical periods can be simplified into the Hindu-Buddhist period, the Islamic period, a brief English and Portuguese period and, most recently, the Dutch period.

Hinduism was introduced to places such as Sumatra, Java, and the South Celebes (Sulawesi) by Indian traders as early as the second century; at the same time, Indian missionaries also brought Buddhism to various parts of Indonesia. The arrival of the

INDONESIAN FLAVORS

latter saw the construction of monuments such as Borobudur, which stands just outside Yogyakarta (the "artistic" capital) in Central Java. Built sometime in the ninth century, it is the largest Buddhist monument in the world. Strangely, Borobudur was abandoned and lost under thick jungle growth almost as soon as it was completed. More than a thousand years later, in 1814, it was rediscovered by an English colonel. The monument was then cleared and renovation began in the mid-1850s.

The fusion of this Indian and Indonesian culture perhaps saw its height in the fourteenth century Javanese Majapahit Empire, which produced extremely rich literature and art forms, including the important *wayang, gamelan,* and batik.

Wayang means "shadow" or "ghost" and is a performance acted out either by real humans or, more usually nowadays, by puppets, usually made out of skin or leather, held up in front of an illuminated screen. A *Wayang Kulit* (an elaborate puppet show) can last for hours and hours, playing out the rich myths and fairy tales which have been handed down for thousands of years.

The term *gamelan* represents a number of instruments of the xylophone family, but most people think of *gamelan* as being the Indonesian gong, which has very ancient origins. A *gamelan* orchestra usually consists of about twelve musicians. For some, the music is an acquired taste. However, inhabitants of Indonesia, especially on

Java and Bali, are accustomed to the sometimes haunting and unearthly sounds which are sometimes described as the sound of moonlight. *Gamelan* is always present at special occasions, but it can also be heard daily in hotel foyers and the like and even in Pasaraya, the large department store in Jakarta.

Batik is the antique art of wax printing on cloth. No one knows quite where it originated, but it is a craft which has always been considered peculiarly Indonesian. Formerly, the wearing of certain designs was limited to royalty and high-ranking officials, and certain colors meant certain things. The colors used were natural organic dyes and so were quite muted and earthy. Nowadays, however, there are thousands of designs and bright colors available, and batik is utilized over a huge spectrum from fashion to interior design.

The fascination and draw of the spices which grow in Indonesia led to the arrival of Arab traders as early as the fourth century. With them came their religion, Islam. This influence has grown to make Indonesia into the largest Muslim nation in the world today, with around 90 percent of the population practicing the religion.

The Portuguese arrived in 1512 and stayed for about 150 years. Their presence was very much a commercial venture, rather than an artistic or cultural one, but there are still many Portuguese words left in the language and there are a few noteworthy buildings still in good repair to be seen. The decline of the Portuguese began in an incident in 1570 when the Sultan of Ternate was murdered, causing them to flee.

The Dutch introduced their East Indies Company (VOC) as early as 1602, a venture which eventually turned into a vast colonial empire. Although Indonesia had

Exquisite, fresh vegetables are a backbone of Indonesian cuisine.

had relations with China from a very early time, many Chinese first arrived during the Dutch occupation to work as coolies. A large number of these, through sheer hard work and perseverance, worked their way up into the merchant classes.

The Dutch exploited Indonesian produce to the full, but they made many contributions, too; they introduced coffee, sugar, pepper, tea, cotton, and indigo, the production of which helped to satisfy the European demand. They also built extensively, and their buildings remain the most impressive in Indonesia.

Meanwhile, during the seventeenth century, the British were the biggest rivals of the Dutch. The control of the East Indies meant the monopoly of an enormously rich source of spices, rubber, rice, soy beans, fish stock, copra, palm oil, bananas, hardwoods, tin, copper, etc., and so competition was fierce. Two hundred years later, in 1811, Stamford Raffles, the well-known founder of Singapore, was appointed as Java's English Administrator, but English control in the region was brief due to squabbles abreast in Europe, and most of the Indies were again handed over to the Dutch in 1816.

The presence and influence of the Dutch was great, but it was inevitable that their imperialism would be challenged by growing Indonesian nationalism. However, it did not find a voice until the Indonesian National Party was created in 1926 and Indonesian independence was sought.

However, other world events intervened: in 1942, the Japanese carried out a full-scale invasion of Sumatra and Java. This saw the end of Dutch power in Indonesia in a humiliatingly short period. Indonesia considered the Japanese to have liberated them from the Dutch, and although their presence was very much a military one, the people have since looked very favorably on Japan. In turn, Japan has always been a large contributor of aid.

Independence was eventually declared by the Indonesian National Party on August 17, 1945. Many obstacles still existed, but the Dutch finally transferred total sovereignty to a free Indonesia on December 27, 1949. The Republic of Indonesia was created with Sukarno as the first President.

Over the following years Indonesia closed in upon itself and became more introspective, looking gravely upon Communism and the West. Events came to a head in the murder of six senior generals in September 1965, rumored to be the work of Communist conspirators. An army reserve was mobilized and total chaos ensued, with mass indiscriminate murder of an enormous number of people. As a result, the

Communist Party was disbanded and the army assumed leadership under the control of Soeharto. The "New Order" saw that the country was subsequently divided into twenty-seven provinces, each headed by a governor nominated by a principal legislature and appointed by the Central Government.

Indonesia is still a poor country with many problems, but its rate of development over the last few years has been extraordinary. By the end of the twentieth century Indonesia will likely be a middle-income country and the trek from poverty may well be nearing its end. The New Order has largely meant positive progress, and the fact that President Soeharto (serving successive terms of five years) has been in power for nearly thirty years has provided essential stability.

To unite so many thousands of island cultures, with differing dialects and beliefs, would be impossible. But with the gradual insistence on the use of one language (Bahasa Indonesia, based on Bahasa Malay), and the importance attached to the state philosophy of the Five Principles *(Pancasila)*—belief in one God; a just and civilized humanity; unity of Indonesia; sovereignty of the people; social justice—relatively civilized rule has prevailed.

A peaceful moment in a small village.

INDONESIAN FLAVORS

QUANTITIES, LIQUIDS, VOLUMES, WEIGHTS, AND TEMPERATURES

Recipes given in this book serve approximately four people. If you wish to serve a more authentic Indonesian meal (which would include possibly four, five, or more dishes), then reduce the ingredients accordingly.

Units of measurement for liquids and volumes in this book are the American tablespoon and cup. The following American-metric-imperial conversion table may be of help.

LIQUIDS AND VOLUMES

American	Metric	Imperial
½ teaspoon	2.5 milliliters	½ teaspoon
1 teaspoon	5 milliliters	1 teaspoon
1 tablespoon	15 milliliters	1 tablespoon
2 tablespoons	30 milliliters	2 tablespoons
3 tablespoons	45 milliliters	3 tablespoons
¼ cup	60 milliliters	4 tablespoons
⅓ cup	75 milliliters	5 tablespoons
6 tablespoons	90 milliliters	6 tablespoons
7 tablespoons	105 milliliters	7 tablespoons
½ cup	125 milliliters	4 fluid ounces
⅔ cup	150 milliliters	¼ pint
¾ cup	175 milliliters	6 fluid ounces
⅞ cup	200 milliliters	⅓ pint
1 cup	150 milliliters	8 fluid ounces
1¼ cups	300 milliliters	½ pint
1½ cups	350 milliliters	12 fluid ounces
1¾ cups	400 milliliters	14 fluid ounces
2 cups	450 milliliters	¾ pint
2¼ cups	500 milliliters	18 fluid ounces
2½ cups	600 milliliters	1 pint
3 cups	750 milliliters	1¼ pints
3¾ cups	900 milliliters	1½ pints
4¼ cups	1 liter	1¾ pints

Meat weight is given in the imperial pound unit of measurement. The following weight conversion chart is approximate for simplification.

WEIGHTS

Ounces/Pounds	Grams
1 ounce	25 grams
4 ounces (¼ pound)	125 grams
8 ounces (½ pound)	250 grams
10 ounces	300 grams
12 ounces (¾ pound)	350 grams
16 ounces (1 pound)	500 grams

NOTE: Small lengths are given in the imperial inch. One centimeter equals approximately ½ inch.

OVEN TEMPERATURES

As noted in the Foreword, Indonesians commonly prepare many dishes and put them out without any regard to keeping them hot; ovens do not really feature in the production of Indonesian food. The flavors of the dish can certainly be appreciated to the full in this way of presentation, but Western taste may still prefer the food at oven or microwave temperatures.

Temperatures for the few dishes that are cooked in an oven in this book are given in degrees Fahrenheit.

Degrees F	Degrees C	Gas Mark
225°	110	¼
250°	130	½
275°	140	1
300°	150	2 (cool)
325°	170	3 (warm)
350°	180	4
375°	190	5 (moderate)
400°	200	6
425°	225	7 (hot)
450°	230	8
475°	240	9 (very hot)

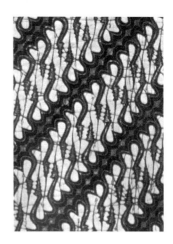

SPECIAL INGREDIENTS, SUBSTITUTES, AND COOKING UTENSILS

Indonesian dishes have the best results if fresh spices and roots are used. Although there are now numerous Southeast Asian and specialist shops for such items, it may be necessary in many cases to use the dried versions. This is perfectly acceptable, and authentic flavors will still be produced. Where even the dried or powdered version of the required item is difficult to obtain, a substitute has been suggested.

Banana *(Pisang)*

Indonesia grows several varieties of banana, most of which are not available in the West. Generally, the largest bananas are the best for use in cooking.

The leaves are also extensively used for temporary plates and as a wrapping during steaming. The original Indonesian take-out (*nasi bungkus,* consisting of a serving of rice and many dishes, usually from a Padang restaurant)·is wrapped up in a pyramid-shaped banana leaf which keeps the enclosed food fresh all day long.

Chili *(Cabe)*

Chili is an essential ingredient in Indonesian cooking, but should not overpower any dish; the potency can easily be diluted if wished. *Cabe rawit* chilies, which are the hottest and come fresh, small, and green, are the best to use, but Indonesians also use the long, thin red and green ones. If a milder dish is required, the seeds can be removed, or the chilies can be soaked in cold water for an hour before required. Dried chilies are generally steamed and then dried. They are not usually as strong as fresh chilies but make an excellent substitute, definitely preferable to the powdered form. Dried chilies should be soaked in warm water before use. Chili sauce (approximately 1 teaspoon per chili) can also be used as a substitute.

Cloves *(Cengkeh)*

Indonesia is the largest producer and importer of the clove. Cloves are mainly used for the *kretek* cigarettes which most Indonesian men smoke, but they are occasionally incorporated into some Indonesian dishes.

Coconut milk *(Santen)*

Coconut milk is one of the ingredients which distinguishes Indonesian cooking from other cuisines, and it is used both as a flavoring and thickening agent. The coconut milk is not the liquid found inside the nut, but rather the juice which is pressed from grated coconut flesh or which comes from dried coconut after it has been soaked in warm water.

Indonesian cooking uses thick, medium, and thin coconut milk. However, it is simpler to standardize and use medium-thickness coconut milk, which is the same thickness found in the canned variety.

Coconut milk made from the fresh nut

> *1 fresh coconut*
> *1½ cups warm water*

Quarter the nut and then grate the flesh into a bowl. Add the water. Squeeze the flesh in the water for a few minutes in order to extract all the milk available from the flesh. The liquid will become pale white. Strain the liquid off and press the pulp to ensure that all the juice has been extracted. It should be used within 8 hours of being made. Canned coconut will keep for up to 1 to 2 days in the refrigerator after opening.

Coconut milk made from dried coconut

> *1 cup dried coconut*
> *2 cups warm water*

Place the coconut in a pan and cover with the water. Allow to soak for 20 minutes and then squeeze the coconut very hard to produce a milky liquid.

When coconut milk has been added to a dish, the dish will need to be constantly stirred at first to avoid separation.

Coconut oil *(Minyak kelapa)*

This is the oil traditionally used in Indonesian cooking, but any vegetable, olive, or corn oil make excellent substitutes.

Coriander *(Ketumbar)*

If possible, buy the coriander seeds and crush them yourself before use. Ground coriander makes a good substitute for fresh. The leaves, also known as Chinese parsley or cilantro, are generally used for garnishing and add a pungent flavor to a dish.

Cumin *(Jintan)*

Cumin is used often but sparingly, as the smell is very strong.

Fermented soybean *(Tempeh)*

Tempeh is distinctly Indonesian and is sold in slabs of about 1-inch thickness and wrapped in banana leaves.

Fishpaste/Balachan *(Terasi)*

Fishpaste is used extensively in Indonesian cooking, but it is perhaps sometimes a little too strong for Western tastes. It is made from shrimp, crab claws, and other seafood, and is used in small amounts as a flavoring, either raw or broiled. Raw *terasi* is ground up with other spices into a thick paste and then fried in a little oil. The smell is overwhelming. Broiled *terasi* is preferable. Omit or substitute with one of the bottled and commercially available fish sauces *(balachan)*.

Galingale *(Langkuas)*

Galingale is a rhizome used in Indonesian cooking, which has a more subtle flavor and smoother texture than ginger. Substitute with the powdered or dried form, which needs to be soaked before use. Its use is generally optional.

Ginger *(Jahe)*

Fresh ginger, peeled and grated, or bruised, should be used if possible; if not, the powdered form makes a satisfactory substitute.

Kaffir lime leaf *(Daun jeruk purut)*

These leaves have a subtle fragrance and are mainly used in lemongrass-based dishes. Substitute with curry or bay leaves. Use 1 bay leaf for every 2 to 3 Kaffir lime leaves.

Lemongrass *(Sereh)*

Lemongrass is used in most curry-based dishes. It is rather like a woody stem of tough grass and can be grown at home. In its fresh form, lemongrass is used either sliced, pounded, or bruised, and it is removed before the dish is served. The topmost, grassiest piece of the stem is discarded before use. Substitute with powdered or dried form but use sparingly. Grated lemon rind can also be used as a substitute, but the flavor is much less subtle.

Lime (*Jeruk*)

These small citrus fruits are used like lemons in the West, which make a good substitute if limes are unavailable or too expensive.

Macadamia (*Kemiri*)

Kemiri is also known as candlenut. It should be roasted before use and is usually ground together with other spices. Use is optional, or substitute with Australian or Hawaiian macadamia nuts or skinned almonds.

Nutmeg (*Pala*)

Once the Banda Islands, the original "Spice Islands" in Indonesia, were the only places on earth where the nutmeg grew on tall majestic, glossy-leafed trees. Banda nutmeg is still recognized as the world's best, but today all that is produced cannot be sold and nutmeg is, somewhat surprisingly, not widely used in Indonesian cooking.

Onion (*Bawang*)

A small, pungent, red-skinned variety is used in Indonesia; it can be satisfactorily substituted for the shallot. Also, the usual French or Spanish onions are perfectly adequate.

Palm sugar (*Gula Jawa*)

This is made from the sap of the yellow coconut flowers and is the usual sweetening agent used in Indonesian cooking. Dark brown sugar makes a good substitute.

Peanuts (*Kacang*)

Peanuts are widely used in Indonesian cooking to contribute to the spicy, slightly sweet taste which is one of the hallmarks of Indonesian food. Raw peanuts are easily found and should be used rather than the poor substitute of peanut butter.

Small dried shrimp (*Ebi*)

These are sundried and then placed in airtight containers. They are usually used as a garnish and so are not absolutely necessary in any dish.

Soy sauce (*Kecap Asin and Kecap Manis*)

Kecap is pronounced "ketchup" and is the Chinese/Indonesian word also used in the

West. *Kecap Asin* is dark and salty; the light colored variety is not used. *Kecap Manis* is distinctly Indonesian. It is thick, black, and sweet and is made from dark soy sauce and molasses.

Tamarind *(Asam)*

The fruit of the tamarind is extracted from relatively large, woody pods. It is dried and looks like a slab of cooking dates when packaged. For use in the following recipes, soak a 2-inch piece of tamarind in approximately 4 tablespoons of hot water for 5 to 10 minutes until it is soft. Squeeze and discard the tamarind, leaving a colored juice. Freshly squeezed lemon juice makes a reasonable substitute.

Tofu *(Tahu)*

Tofu is a soft white bean curd available in Chinese groceries, specialty shops, health food stores, and increasingly in many supermarkets.

Turmeric *(Kunyit)*

Turmeric is an essential root in Indonesian cooking. Substitute with powdered or dried form.

Utensils

Very few adjustments need to be made to the standard kitchen for successful Indonesian cooking. The only two items which are totally essential are a *wajan* (wok), and either a blender or electric grinder, or an *ulekan* (Indonesian stone mortar, or any type of mortar and pestle) for blending and grinding the spices.

A RESTAURANT TOUR OF JAKARTA

In order to appreciate how varied Indonesian dishes can be, a visit to a few of Jakarta's *rumah makan* (eating houses) is very worthwhile. The menus listed also provide a sense of the number of dishes served at one meal and the type of foods which are mixed. Some of the dishes seen here are included in the following appropriate chapters as indicated.

The *Warung*

These unbelievably abundant, compact, and mobile "restaurants" or roadside stalls and the various cooking smells which emanate from them, are perhaps the first and most lingering impression made on visitors to Indonesia. *Warungs* typically serve dishes such as *soto* (soup), *satay*, *nasi goreng* (fried rice), *pisang goreng* (fried bananas), *tempe*, (fermented bean curd) and a host of vegetables and tubers cooked in batters.

The locals know when their favorite meal or snack is around as each "restaurateur" makes a distinctive noise (either a certain shout, the tinkling of a bell, or the knocking of a piece of wood against the stall) when approaching the area in which they wish to set up shop and serve food.

Warung food superbly illustrates the casual but expert approach to food in Indonesia and its communal nature.

The following *warung* foods included in this book are:

Keripik Tempe	Crisp-fried Bean Curd
Satay	Barbecued Meat on Wooden Skewers
Martabak	Beef-stuffed Savory Pancakes
Pisang Goreng	Fried Bananas

Food Alfresco at Jalan Pecenongan

Jalan Pecenongan, a street in the center of Jakarta, shows how Indonesians like their food to be prepared on the spot and consumed immediately. The food is delicious because of its freshness, the immediacy of preparation, and the method of cooking. Masses of vegetables are used, and the ingredients are stir-fried very quickly, making this form of preparation a good example of the Chinese influence on typical Indonesian cuisine.

Yet it is a slightly bizarre scene: during the day, the street is lined with shops and offices, but by about 6:30 p.m. everything has been transformed by the addition of mobile stalls, makeshift restaurants, street entertainers, and hawkers. Around midnight everything vanishes again, as though it had never been there.

At the Along Restaurant we enjoyed the following menu (recipes for these dishes are included in the book):

Sop Asparagus dan Kepiting	Crab and Asparagus Soup
Hot Plate Kangkung	Steamed Spinach with Pigeon's Eggs
Ikan Gurame di Goreng Kering	Crispy-fried Pomfret Fish
Udang Rebus	Steamed Prawns
Bakmi Goreng	Fried Noodles

The Padang Restaurant

Padang food (originating in the town of that name in Western Sumatra) is very popular in Indonesia. The food is typically seen stacked up in the windows of the restaurants in neatly patterned rows of dishes. The customer points to which dishes he or she wishes to be served and then only pays for what is eaten. None of these would be hot, and dishes sometimes consist of offal and other items which might not be so appealing to Westerners.

However, Padang food provided one of the first "restaurant" methods of presenting food in Indonesia, a forerunner of the "fast food" idea, and it is still very much part of Indonesian daily life. The style contributes some major and exquisite dishes to the cuisine such as the spicy *Rendang Daging Sapi* (beef cubes, or more traditionally buffalo, cooked in coconut milk). The best way to make a meal of this dish is to serve it with plain boiled rice and, a little untraditionally, a simple green salad.

The Sundanese Restaurant

These canteen-style restaurants, specializing in typically Javanese food, abound all over Jakarta. They are excellent for the variety of dishes available at a very reasonable cost, the freshness of the food (the fish swim in ponds and specially made waterways in the actual restaurants), and the swiftness with which the food is served.

The Raden Kuring Restaurant is a well known Sundanese restaurant in Jakarta and nightly presents excellent food which can be eaten to the music played for traditional *Jaipongan* dancers. Sundanese restaurants provide an extremely good opportunity to savor the many types of fish found in Indonesia, and the various methods of cooking them. We enjoyed the menu below; all these dishes are described herein:

Sayur Asam	Traditional Indonesian Sour Vegetable Soup
Nasi Goreng	Fried Rice
Ikan Gurame di Goreng Kering	Crispy-fried Pomfret Fish
Ikan Bakar	Barbecued Fish
Acar Ketimun	Cucumber Pickle
Karedok	Raw Vegetable Salad with Spicy Peanut Dressing
Sambal Cobek	Chili and Shrimp Paste on a Stone Plate

Nyonya Suharti Rumah Makan

If one of the many fast food restaurants of the West wanted to improve its recipe for fried chicken, the cooks might first look to this restaurant. Originally set up in Yogyakarta in Central Java, the restaurant is also well known for its traditional Yogya dish of *Gudeg*, an unusual combination of jackfruit and chicken. The following would be a very typical Indonesian menu:

Nasi Putih	Steamed Rice
Ayam Goreng Besar	Large Fried Chicken from Yogyakarta
Gudeg	Chicken and Jackfruit Casserole from Yogyakarta
Gado Gado	Steamed Vegetables with Peanut Sauce

Rijsttafel (Rice Table)

The Oasis Restaurant

This is a restaurant very much in its own class, illustrating the way in which Indonesia's colonial settlers adapted Indonesian food to suit their own tastes and subsequently created new and fascinating ways of serving food.

The restaurant is situated in the old Dutch area of Menteng. It was originally a house built in 1928 in the Raffles-period style by a Dutch millionaire who owned tea, rubber, and cinchona estates. The atmosphere is delightfully reminiscent of an age of colonial elegance and splendor, heightened by the artifacts and works of art displayed in the restaurant. Guests are appropriately welcomed by the striking of an enormous Sundanese *gamelan*.

The house became a restaurant in the 1970s, and although an impressive and extensive a la carte menu is served, it is for the exclusive Dutch *Rijsttafel* (Rice Table) that the Oasis is primarily known. This is the name given to a method of presenting food which the Dutch took from the Indonesian custom of serving many dishes at once.

A unique flair is added by a procession of twelve pretty girls wearing traditional dress and carrying the food on Ming-style pottery plates *(piring batu)*. This is how the *Rijsttafel* would have been served in the large colonial homes and palaces of Batavia, the old Dutch name for Jakarta.

The *Rijsttafel* has been perfected since 1979 at The Oasis by Ibu Malia Soenario — a woman now in her eighties — who presides over the kitchen. Ibu Malia Soenario gained enviable expertise in the various cuisines of the world at a very early age when her father was Regent of Bandung and entertained a host of cosmopolitan guests.

The following would make for a typical *Rijstaffel*, celebration menu (asterisks indicate the dishes included in the book):

Soto Bandung	Traditional Soup from Bandung
*Nasi Putih**	Steamed White Rice
*Omelet Kepiting**	Crab Omelet
Ikan Gulai Masin	Fish Fillets in Turmeric Sauce
*Gulai Kambing**	Spicy Lamb or Mutton Curry
*Ayam Goreng**	Fried Chicken
*Satay Kambing dan Sapi**	Lamb and Beef Satay
*Orak Arik Jagung Muda**	Stewed Baby Corn
Sambal Goreng Tempe	Sweet Soybean Cake
*Serundeng**	Fried Grated Coconut with Peanuts
*Pisang Goreng**	Fried Banana
Emping	Nut Crackers
Acar Bening	Clear Pickles
*Sambal Ulek**	Fresh Ground Red Chilies
Sambal Bajak	Fried Chilies with Shrimp Paste

SOP DAN SOTO

SOUPS

Soups in Indonesia are not traditionally served as a separate course, but are put out along with everything else; often they are just poured over the rice or noodles to make the food pleasantly moist and tasty.

Indonesian soups are generally like consommé: a stock filled with meat, fish, and vegetables. *Soto*, however, is generally thicker than *sop*.

SOTO AYAM
Chicken Soup

Soups made of chicken are found everywhere in Indonesia. *Soto Ayam* is one of the dishes always to be found in an Indonesian restaurant abroad.

> 1 chicken weighing about 2 pounds
> Approximately 2 tablespoons vegetable oil for frying
> 5 scallions, finely sliced
> 2 tablespoons dark soy sauce
> 1 tablespoon white vinegar
> 1 cup bean sprouts
> ¾ cup crisp fried potato slices
> ½ cup cellophane noodles, soaked briefly in hot water until softened and then put aside to drain
> 4 hard-cooked eggs, cut into quarters
> 2 tablespoons crispy fried shallots and 1 tablespoon chopped coriander, or parsley leaves, to garnish

SPICE PASTE:

1-inch piece fresh ginger, crushed

6 cloves garlic, crushed

1 teaspoon freshly ground black pepper

Salt to taste

Boil the chicken in water to cover until tender. Reserve approximately 6 cups of the stock. Bone the chicken and shred into small pieces. Stir-fry the chicken pieces in oil until golden and set aside.

Grind the ingredients for the spice paste in a mortar and pestle, or place in blender and mix until smooth. Fry the spice paste until fragrant and then add to the stock and bring the mixture to a boil. Add the scallions, soy sauce, and vinegar. Mix well, adjust seasoning with salt, and simmer for a few minutes.

Arrange some of the chicken, bean sprouts, fried potato, cellophane noodles, and hard-cooked eggs in the bottom of individual soup bowls. Pour the stock over these and garnish with the shallots and the coriander leaves.

Alternatively, serve the stock in a large jug and arrange the other ingredients on a large platter for the guests to create their own servings of *Soto Ayam.*

SERVES 4.

MIE AYAM GODOG
Noodles in Chicken Soup

The chicken in this soup can easily be replaced by equal amounts of shrimp, fish, or meat.

Approximately 3 tablespoons vegetable oil for frying

4 shallots (or 1 small onion) finely sliced

3 cloves garlic, crushed

4 cups water

1-inch piece fresh ginger, grated

2 chicken breasts, skinned

½ small cabbage, shredded

3 fresh red chilies, finely chopped (or 3 dried chilies or 2 teaspoons chili powder)

3 scallions, chopped

¼ cup bean sprouts

1½ cups Chinese egg noodles

2 tablespoons dark soy sauce

Salt and freshly ground black pepper, to taste

Crispy fried shallots, hard-cooked egg slices or thick strips of omelet, and chopped coriander or
parsley leaves, to garnish

Heat the oil in a wok and add the shallots and garlic. Stir-fry for a few minutes and then add the water, ginger, and chicken.

Bring the mixture to a boil and then simmer for about 30 minutes or until the chicken is tender.

Remove the chicken from the pan and bone and shred the meat, leaving the stock over a low heat to continue simmering.

Add the cabbage leaves, chilies, and shredded chicken. Bring the mixture to a gentle boil and then add the scallions, bean sprouts, and noodles. Stir in the soy sauce.

Adjust the seasoning, adding salt and pepper to taste, cover and simmer for about 7 minutes or until the noodles are cooked. Garnish and serve.

SERVES 4.

SOP UDANG

Shrimp Soup

¾ cup rice vermicelli

Approximately 2 tablespoons vegetable oil for frying

6 shallots (or 1 medium onion), thinly sliced

3 cloves garlic, crushed

2-inch piece fresh ginger, grated

1 teaspoon coriander seeds, crushed

1 teaspoon turmeric

2 cups water or any fish stock

1 cup coconut milk (see Special Ingredients section)

1 cup shrimp, cleaned and heads removed but left unpeeled

½ cup bean sprouts

Salt and freshly ground black pepper, to taste

4 scallions, chopped, to garnish

Put the vermicelli into a saucepan and pour over enough boiling water to cover. Set aside for about 5 minutes and then strain.

Heat the oil in a wok and fry the shallots and garlic for a few minutes. Add the ginger, coriander, and turmeric. Add the water (or stock) and simmer for about 30 minutes.

Add the vermicelli and the coconut milk and gently simmer the mixture. Add the shrimp and bean sprouts and continue to simmer for a further 5 minutes. Adjust the seasoning, adding salt and pepper to taste, and garnish with the scallions.

SERVES 4.

SAYUR ASAM
Sour Vegetable Soup

4 shallots (or 1 small onion) finely chopped

3 cloves garlic, crushed

3 fresh small red chilies, finely chopped (or 3 dried chilies or 2 teaspoons chili powder)

2 Kaffir lime leaves (or 1 bay leaf)

1 large potato, cleaned but left unpeeled and chopped into segments

2½ cups chicken stock

½ cup string beans, chopped into 1-inch lengths

2 zucchini, sliced

½ small cabbage, shredded

2-inch piece tamarind soaked for 10 minutes in 4 tablespoons hot water and then squeezed and discarded to leave a colored juice (or 4 tablespoons lime or lemon juice)

Salt and freshly ground black pepper, to taste

½ cup peanuts, roasted

Place shallots, garlic, chilies, Kaffir lime leaves, potatoes, and stock into a large saucepan.

Bring the mixture to a boil and then simmer for approximately 7 minutes.

Add the beans and simmer for a few minutes before adding the zucchini; simmer for a further 3 minutes. Add the cabbage, tamarind water, and adjust seasoning, adding salt and pepper to taste.

Simmer for a further 5 minutes or until vegetables are cooked but still crunchy. Add the peanuts. Discard Kaffir lime leaves before serving.

SERVES 4.

SAYUR DENGAN SANTEN
Vegetables in Coconut Milk

Approximately 4 tablespoons vegetable oil for frying
4 shallots (or 1 small onion), finely chopped
3 cloves garlic, crushed
2 fresh red chilies (or 2 dried chilies or 2 teaspoons chili powder)
1 stalk lemongrass, bruised (or 1 teaspoon grated lemon rind or ½ teaspoon powdered form)
1 cup water or chicken stock
1 cup coconut milk (see Special Ingredients section)
½ cup string beans cut into 1-inch lengths
½ cup mushrooms, roughly chopped
½ small cabbage, shredded
½ cup bean sprouts
Salt and freshly ground black pepper, to taste

Heat the oil in a wok, and add the shallots and garlic and fry for a few minutes. Add the chilies and lemongrass and stir well.

Add the water (or stock) and the coconut milk and bring to a boil, stirring continuously. Add the beans and continue cooking for a few minutes. Add the mushrooms and the cabbage and continue to simmer. Finally, add the bean sprouts and cook for a few minutes longer until the vegetables are cooked but still crunchy.

Adjust seasoning, adding salt and pepper to taste, discard lemongrass and serve.

SERVES 4.

SAYUR BAYAM
Spinach Soup

4 shallots (or 1 small onion), finely sliced
2 fresh green chilies, finely chopped (or 2 dried chilies or 1 teaspoon chili powder)
3 tablespoons dark soy sauce
1 cup water
1 Kaffir lime leaf (or 1 small bay leaf)
1 teaspoon ground turmeric
Salt and freshly ground black pepper, to taste

1 pound spinach, washed and roughly chopped
½ cup garden peas (or frozen peas)

Place shallots, chilies, soy sauce, water, Kaffir lime leaf, and ground turmeric into a large saucepan. Bring the mixture to a boil, cover and simmer for 10 minutes.

Add the spinach and more water if necessary, and then add the garden peas. Continue to simmer for a further 7 minutes. Discard the Kaffir lime leaf, adjust seasoning, adding salt and pepper to taste, and serve hot.

SERVES 4.

SOP IKAN PEDAS
Spicy Hot Fish Soup

1 pound cod or other firm, white fish, cleaned and left whole
1 tablespoon lime (or lemon) juice

SPICE PASTE:
6 shallots (or 1 small onion), roughly chopped
3 cloves garlic, crushed
2 fresh green chilies, chopped (or 2 dried chilies or 2 teaspoons chili powder)
1-inch piece fresh ginger, crushed
1 teaspoon ground turmeric

Approximately 1 tablespoon vegetable oil for frying
1 stalk lemongrass, bruised
1-inch piece fresh ginger, crushed
1 Kaffir lime leaf (or 1 small bay leaf)
2 cups water
Salt and freshly ground black pepper, to taste
Chopped coriander or parsley leaves, to garnish

Rub the lime juice into the fish and allow to stand for about 15 minutes.

Grind the ingredients for the spice paste in a mortar and pestle, or place in blender and mix until smooth. Heat the oil and fry the paste, lemongrass, ginger, and Kaffir lime leaf.

Add the water and bring to a boil. Add the fish and simmer for approximately half an hour or until the fish is tender.

Discard lemongrass and Kaffir lime leaf, and adjust seasoning with salt and pepper to taste, garnish, and serve.

SERVES 4.

SOTO DENGAN KEPITING DAN ASPARAGUS
Crab and Asparagus Soup

Approximately 2 tablespoons vegetable oil for frying
6 shallots (or 1 medium onion), thinly sliced
1 tablespoon sugar
1 cup young asparagus, chopped
1 fresh red chili, very finely chopped (or 1 dried chili or ½ teaspoon chili powder)
1-inch piece fresh ginger, grated
1 tablespoon dark soy sauce
2 cups chicken stock
1 cup crab meat (white meat only-can be fresh, frozen, or canned)
Salt and freshly ground black pepper, to taste
1 tablespoon chopped coriander or parsley leaves, 3 scallions, sliced, to garnish

Heat the oil in a wok and fry the shallots for a few minutes.

Add the sugar and stir continuously for a further 2 minutes.

Add the asparagus, chili, ginger, and soy sauce.

Add the stock and bring to a boil. Simmer the mixture for approximately 25 minutes. Stir in the crab meat and simmer for a few more minutes. Adjust the seasoning, adding salt and pepper to taste, and garnish with the coriander or parsley leaves and scallions.

SERVES 4.

(Above): Roadside refreshments from young coconuts. (Right): Fresh fish ready for the pot. (Below): A sampling of beautiful marketplace produce.

(Above): Mountains of chilis. Shrimps, (right), and all types of small dried fish lend flavor to Indonesian food.

(Above): Kunyit — tumeric — the root with the most distinctive "earthy" aroma.
(Right): Bawang — the Indonesian onion. (Below): No part of the magnificent
banana is wasted: the flower is edible, and the leaves are used as plates, table mats,
cooking tools, and many other things.

(This page): Fresh tempeh, fish, and coconuts—all staples of Indonesian cuisine.
(Opposite page, top left): The pete *bean. (Top right): Lush local produce. (Bottom): Vendors display bunches of lichee nuts at the Rambutan.*

(This page, top): Cool ice for hot days and hot dishes. Large blocks of ice are produced in all market places and have numerous uses. They can often be seen perched precariously on the backs of bicycles, the rider hurriedly pedaling to his destination before his purchase disappears in the heat. (Below): Everywhere, fields are terraced to maximize arable land.

*A Rijstaffel feast (left) served
with flair at the Oasis restaurant
by a procession of traditionally
dressed women.*

(Right): Chilies. (Below): The water buffalo is not only an important source of meat but is still used extensively for plowing the fields.

(Above): Sirasak, *coconuts.*
(Left): Pineapples.

INDONESIAN FLAVORS

(Above): The Nyonga Suharti Rumah Makan *serves chicken at its finest.*
(Right): Sundanese restaurant favorites.

(Opposite page, top): The Padang
restaurant serves fast food at a glance.
(Below): Typical Padang spread.
(This page, top): Fast and furious work.
(Below left): Fresh fish.
(Below right): Steamy fresh smells
wafting from a wok.

(Oppostie page, top): Tasty banana fritters. (Bottom): Warungs serve a host of vegetables and tubers cooked in batters.

(This page, top): The durian.

(Bottom): Tempeh and tofu are very popular ingredients with the Warung.

(Above): Typical Warung fare.
(Below): An abundance of fresh flavors.

INDONESIAN FLAVORS

NASI DAN MIE
RICE AND NOODLES

Rice is the staple food of Indonesia, and numerous varieties are grown, including red and black grain strains. In many places, especially on islands such as Bali, it is breathtaking to see how every piece of land is put to the use of creating rice paddies; even the steepest hills seem to have been terraced. The paddies also provide additional food in the way of the fresh water shrimp and ducks that make their homes in these congenial surroundings.

Long grain rice is used in all the following recipes. The Indonesians like to make use of glutinous varieties as well, for unusual dishes and for puddings. Not surprisingly, because rice is a staple food in Indonesia, hundreds of novel ways have been devised to cook it, and in unusual containers, too, such as bamboo tubes and woven coconut leaf pouches. Rice is traditionally eaten with the fingers of the right hand (as Indonesia is largely a Muslim country, the left hand is considered unclean). Until very recently, most food was eaten this way.

Noodles, although associated more with Chinese cooking, are also an important part of Indonesian cuisine. They can be homemade but, like pasta, it is probably much simpler and more satisfactory to buy them pre-made with either wheat or rice flour and with or without eggs.

Plain White Rice (*Nasi Putih*)
Cooked rice should always be fluffy and easy to separate. To achieve this, the best way to cook the rice is to parboil it for about 5 minutes and then steam it for the rest of the cooking time. A colander with the lid set over a saucepan of water is perfectly

adequate for this second process.

It is difficult to estimate just how much rice people will eat, but a general guide is about ¼ cup per person, measured with 1 volume of water per 1 volume of rice. 1–1½ cups of rice should therefore very generously serve 4 people.

To make, wash and drain 1 cup rice.

Boil 1 cup water in a large saucepan and add a little oil when it has come to a boil (salt is not added to rice in Indonesian cooking). Add the rice. Cover and boil for approximately 5 minutes. Drain.

Place drained rice in colander and place over saucepan which has enough water to steam the rice. Steam until fluffy but still firm in the center, then serve.

SERVES 4.

Fried Rice (*Nasi Goreng*)

This dish is synonymous with Indonesian food and is eaten at any time of the day: for breakfast, lunch, or dinner, where it can be a main course or an accompaniment. *Nasi Goreng* is really open to any interpretation and can be as simple or elaborate as desired, with added meat and fish and garnishes of cucumber, tomato, fried shallots, hard-cooked eggs or fried eggs, or strips of omelet. The most elaborate *Nasi Goreng* is usually known as *Nasi Goreng Istimewa.*

One accompaniment which is always present is the *krupuk,* wafers made from prawns or various nuts; *krupuk* can be purchased in any Chinese grocery store or specialty shop. *Nasi Goreng* is always best eaten with a spicy relish (page 49–54).

This dish is excellent for using up leftovers and is very easy and quick to prepare. The rice, however, should be cooked at least two hours in advance of this dish.

1½ cups cooked and cooled long grain rice
Approximately 3 tablespoons vegetable oil for frying
6 shallots (or 1 medium onion), finely chopped
2 cloves garlic, crushed and finely chopped
3 fresh red chilies, chopped (or 3 dried chilies or 2 teaspoons chili powder)
2 teaspoons dark soy sauce
A dash of dark brown sugar
A dash of salt and freshly ground black pepper
Garnish as desired

After preparing the rice, heat the oil in a wok and add the shallots, garlic, and chilies. Add the rice, soy sauce, and sugar and adjust the seasoning with salt and pepper to taste. Combine and stir well and cook for about 5 to 6 minutes. If the mixture becomes too dry, add some water or even a beaten egg.

Remove from the heat and serve on a large plate; garnish as desired.

SERVES 4.

The Indonesian people love any excuse for a celebration of any kind—birthdays, weddings, anniversaries, and even funerals—any occasion that provides a chance for everyone to get together. Even when there isn't much money to spare, somehow the celebrations seem to be very large and elaborate affairs. At weddings it is not unusual for there to be more than 500 guests. In the *kampungs* (locals' villages) a canopied area will signify just where the celebration is to take place, and the roadside leading to the party will be attractively decorated with skillfully woven and carved palm fronds.

Idul Fitri (the festival to mark the end of the month of fasting at *Ramadan*) is perhaps one of the largest and most celebrated occasions. People exchange gifts and there is a mass exodus from cities like Jakarta, whose inhabitants return to their villages all over Indonesia in order to be with their families and to enjoy all their favorite dishes. Many prior arrangements and plans have to be made to orchestrate these affairs.

Up in northern Sulawesi, the Torajan people, who practice a very unusual mixture of Christianity and animism, sometimes have to make preparations many years in advance for a funeral.

Traditionally, when a member of a noble family in the area died, an elaborate funeral ceremony would take place, usually held over a number of days, culminating in the slaughter of a relatively rare type of buffalo. The richer the family, the more buffalo (as well as pigs) would be slaughtered. The deceased body would then be precariously hauled up onto the rocks to be placed in a chamber specially hewn out for it. An effigy of the deceased would adorn the outside of the chamber in the rocks.

The ceremony still continues today, but the Torajan people have to put together a colossal amount of money to buy the necessary buffalo. So sometimes a body will be preserved and kept in the family's house for a number of years. When the funeral finally takes place, it is a real cause for celebration and not particularly somber.

The dish below is an attractive and simple one and is very much associated with the celebrations and festivities which take place in Indonesia year long. It is often served decoratively in the shape of a cone.

NASI KUNING
Yellow Rice

1½ cups long grain rice
2 cups coconut milk (see Special Ingredients section)
2 teaspoons ground turmeric
1 Kaffir lime leaf (or 1 small bay leaf)
2 cloves
Salt and freshly ground black pepper, to taste
2 large red chilies, de-seeded and cut into long strips, to garnish

Soak the rice in cold water for 1 hour. Wash and drain it and place in a saucepan with the coconut milk and all other ingredients.

Boil the mixture until all the coconut milk has been absorbed.

Steam for approximately 8 minutes. Discard Kaffir lime leaf and cloves. Adjust seasoning adding salt and pepper. Garnish with the red chilies, and serve.

SERVES 4.

Other favorite rice dishes served during celebrations are the popular *Lontong* (Compressed Boiled Rice), and its variation, *Ketupat.* They are both basically solid blocks of boiled or steamed rice, the latter being the most attractive as the rice is cooked in little woven cubes of young coconut or palm leaves.

The dishes can be reproduced by cooking the rice sealed and immersed in boiling water for at least 1 hour, left to cool, and then sliced. They make an interesting variation to eating separated rice in a bowl.

NASI BUMBU
Spicy Rice

1½ cups long grain rice, washed and drained

SPICE PASTE:
2 tablespoons coriander seeds, crushed

2 tablespoons cumin seeds (or 1½ tablespoons ground cumin)

2-inch piece fresh ginger, crushed

2 teaspoons ground turmeric

Approximately 3 tablespoons vegetable oil for frying

¾ pound chicken, cut into small pieces

3 cloves

1-inch stick cinnamon (or 1 teaspoon ground cinnamon)

1 stalk lemongrass, bruised (or 1 teaspoon grated lemon rind or ½ teaspoon powdered form)

2 Kaffir lime leaves (or 1 bay leaf)

3 cups coconut milk (see Special Ingredients section)

2 hard-cooked eggs, shelled

3 potatoes, peeled and chopped into quarters

Salt and freshly ground black pepper, to taste

Steam the rice until half cooked.

Grind the ingredients for the spice paste in a mortar and pestle, or place in blender and mix until smooth.

Heat the oil in a wok and fry the spice paste until fragrant. Add the chicken, cloves, cinnamon, lemongrass, and Kaffir lime leaves. Stir well and add the coconut milk.

Cook until the chicken is tender, add the half-cooked rice, and continue cooking until all the water has been absorbed by the rice. Mix the hard-cooked eggs and potatoes into the rice and steam until the mixture is done. Discard the cinnamon, lemongrass, and Kaffir lime leaves before serving.

SERVES 4.

SAVORY ROLLS OF STUFFED RICE

Arem-arem

1½ cups long grain rice
2 cups coconut milk (see Special Ingredients section)
2 Kaffir lime leaves
Approximately 2 tablespoons vegetable oil for frying

SPICE PASTE:
1 tomato, finely chopped

2 teaspoons ground turmeric

A dash of salt and freshly ground black pepper

A dash of dark brown sugar

STUFFING:

6 shallots (or 1 medium onion), finely chopped

2 cloves garlic, crushed and finely chopped

3 fresh red chilies, finely sliced (or 3 dried chilies or 2 teaspoons chili powder)

2 teaspoons ground turmeric

1 Kaffir lime leaf (or 1 bay leaf)

½ pound minced beef filet

1 cup coconut milk (see Special Ingredients section)

Banana leaves or aluminum foil

Place the rice and coconut milk into a saucepan, and add the Kaffir lime leaves. Boil until the coconut milk has been absorbed by the rice and the grains are tender but still firm in the center. Discard Kaffir lime leaves and set aside.

Heat the oil in a wok and fry the mixed spice paste with the stuffing ingredients —shallots, garlic, chilies, turmeric, and Kaffir lime leaf.

Add the beef and stir-fry until the meat has changed color. Add the coconut milk and simmer the mixture until the beef is tender and the coconut milk has been almost completely absorbed.

Take a piece of banana leaf or aluminum foil and place on it 2 tablespoons of the rice. Flatten the rice and add 2 teaspoons of the meat mixture on top. Enclose the filling with another 2 tablespoons of rice.

Roll the banana leaf or foil into a roll. Secure the ends tightly.

Repeat the process with the rest of the mixture; then steam the rolls for about 30 minutes.

SERVES 4.

BAKMI GORENG
Fried Noodles

This dish is almost as popular as *Nasi Goreng,* and various ingredients can be added to make it as substantial or snack-like as desired.

Approximately 6 tablespoons vegetable oil for frying

6 scallions, chopped

2 cloves garlic, crushed

½ pound minced beef filet

1 cup cooked shrimp or ½ pound cooked chicken cut into strips

Salt and freshly ground black pepper, to taste

4 tablespoons dark soy sauce

2 cups cooked Chinese egg noodles

1 cup bean sprouts or ½ small cabbage, sliced

4 tomatoes, sliced

4 sticks celery, sliced

4 eggs

4 fresh red chilies, seeded and sliced, to garnish

Heat approximately 2 tablespoons of the oil in a wok and fry the scallions. Add the garlic, minced beef, shrimp, or chicken strips, salt and pepper to taste, and soy sauce. When the minced beef is cooked, set aside.

Heat approximately another 2 tablespoons oil in a wok and stir in the noodles. When the noodles are hot, stir in the prepared meat and shrimp. Combine well and then add the sliced vegetables.

Keep stirring until very hot. Break the eggs over the top, garnish with the sliced chilies, and serve immediately.

SERVES 4.

KETOPRAK

Noodles with Salad and Tofu

1 cup cooked rice vermicelli

1 cup bean sprouts, parboiled for 3 minutes and drained

Approximately 12 squares of fried tofu cubes

¼ cup cooked shrimp

4 shallots (or 1 small onion), fried until brown and crispy

2 stalks celery, sliced

Arrange all ingredients on large platter and serve with a peanut sauce as described for *Gado Gado* (see page 55).

SERVES 4.

MIHUN INSTAN
Instant Vermicelli

This is as versatile as any other rice and noodle dish mentioned. Various combinations of meat or fish and vegetables can be used, or simply vegetables. Like *Ketoprak* above, it makes a very quick and satisfying dish.

> *1 cup rice vermicelli*
> *Approximately 2 tablespoons vegetable oil for frying*
> *6 shallots (or 1 medium onion), finely sliced*
> *2 teaspoons coriander seeds, crushed*
> *1-inch piece fresh ginger, grated*
> *2 chicken breasts, skinned, boned and chopped into small pieces*
> *3 medium carrots, chopped*
> *½ small cabbage, shredded*
> *2 tablespoons dark soy sauce*
> *4 scallions, chopped*
> *¾ cup shrimp, cooked and peeled*
> *Salt and freshly ground black pepper, to taste*

Pour boiling water over the rice vermicelli and leave to stand for a few minutes. Wash the vermicelli under running cold water and then leave to drain.

Heat the oil in a wok and fry the shallots for a few minutes. Add the coriander and ginger and continue cooking for a minute before adding the chicken, carrots, and cabbage. Continue cooking for about 5 minutes.

Add the soy sauce and vermicelli and then add the scallions and shrimp.

Adjust seasoning with salt and pepper to taste, and continue cooking for a few more minutes. Serve immediately.

SERVES 4.

SAMBALS, ACAR, AND IRINGAN

RELISHES, PICKLES, AND ACCOMPANIMENTS

Some of the Indonesian relishes—*sambals*—are extremely powerful and their character can best be summed up in the use of the Indonesian word *pedas* (i.e., extremely spicy-hot). However, their fiery nature can obviously be subdued to suit varying tastes.

A *sambal* is very important to an Indonesian meal and is usually served on small stone dishes and garnished with a tiny lime, *jeruk limo.* The spicy peanut sauce used in *Gado Gado* can also be used as a *sambal.* Most *sambals* keep well for a week or more in sealed containers in the refrigerator, so the amounts that some of the following recipes produce would be sufficient for more than one meal.

Pickles provide a refreshing and clean-tasting contrast to all the heat and spice of relishes, and they are served in a similar manner to those found in Indian food, in small dishes throughout the meal.

Indonesian meals are almost never complete without accompaniments such as crispy fried onions, sliced hard-cooked eggs, or simply fried peanuts. Either *krupuk* (prawn crackers), *emping* (small, bitter crisps made from the melinjo nut), or *kripik kentang* (simply crisp fried potato slices) also make an appearance. There are more unusual accompaniments, too, and one of the tastiest is *serundeng*, which is included here and which could almost be eaten as a snack in itself.

KECAP MANIS
Sweet Ketchup

This is a good base for many relishes and sauces and may not be available in the shops.

3 tablespoons molasses or dark brown sugar
¾ cup dark soy sauce

Simply dissolve the sugar in the soy sauce.

SERVES 4.

SAMBAL ULEK OR SAMBAL COBEK
Crushed Chilies

This is the quintessential "hot" *sambal;* its name is derived from the Indonesian implement for grinding spices the *ulek ulek,* which crushes ingredients in the *cobek.* A blender simplifies the process.

1 cup fresh red chilies (or equivalent dried chilies, chili powder is not suitable in this sambal)
2 teaspoons salt
A little water

Grind ingredients in mortar and pestle, or place in blender and mix until fairly smooth.

SERVES 12.

SAMBAL KECAP
Chili and Soy Sauce

6 tablespoons dark soy sauce
2 fresh red chilies, cut up into small circles (or 2 dried chilies or 1 teaspoon chili powder)
3 small fresh green chilies, cut up into small circles
3 shallots (or one small onion), finely diced
2 tablespoons lime (or lemon) juice
2 cloves garlic, crushed and finely chopped

Place all ingredients in a small saucepan and cook over a moderately low heat for approximately 5 minutes, stirring constantly.

This sauce adds an excellent taste when poured over plain rice.

SERVES 4.

SAMBAL TERASI
Shrimp Paste Relish

Because of the smell and pungent taste of the *terasi* (see Special Ingredients section for description) this relish is for the acquired taste. It should be made in small quantities as, unlike most other relishes, it does not keep well.

> 6 fresh small green chilies
> 3 shallots (or ½ small onion)
> 2 cloves garlic
> Juice of 1 lime (or ½ lemon)
> 1 slice broiled terasi
> A dash of salt

Fry the chilies for a few minutes and then grind them together with the shallots, garlic and lime juice, or place in blender and mix until relatively smooth.

Combine this mixture with the terasi and adjust seasoning.

SERVES 4.

SAMBAL TOMAT CABE
Tomato Chili Sauce

> 4 large fresh red chilies (or 4 dried chilies, or, as a very last resort, 4 teaspoons chili powder)
> Approximately 4 tablespoons vegetable oil for frying
> 10 shallots (or 2 medium-sized onions), finely sliced
> 3 cloves garlic, crushed
> 2 tablespoons tomato paste
> 1 teaspoon dark brown sugar
> Salt and freshly ground black pepper to taste

Slice the chilies into thin strips and discard the seeds if a mild sauce is required.

Heat the oil in a small pan and fry the shallots and garlic until the shallots are transparent. Reduce heat and add the chilies and cook for approximately 10 minutes.

Add the tomato paste, sugar, and a little water and cook until the sauce has thickened. Adjust seasoning, adding salt and pepper to taste; serve hot or cold.

SERVES 4.

ACAR KETIMUN
Cucumber Pickle

1 large cucumber, washed but preferably left unpeeled
1 tablespoon salt
¾ cup vinegar (either white or malt)
1 teaspoon caster sugar
2 fresh red chilies, finely chopped, or ground (or 2 dried chilies or 1½ teaspoon chili powder)
Salt and freshly ground black pepper to taste

Halve and quarter the cucumber lengthwise and then cut into approximately 1-inch lengths and place into a colander. Sprinkle with salt and leave for about 15 minutes. Rinse and drain the cucumber.

Heat the vinegar and then dissolve the sugar in it. Combine the cucumber, vinegar mixture, and chilies in a bowl while still warm. Season with salt and pepper and allow to cool before serving.

SERVES 4 TO 6.

ACAR BUAH SAYUR
Mixed Vegetable Pickle

1 large cucumber, washed (but left unpeeled) and halved and quartered lengthwise and then cut into 1-inch lengths
1 large carrot, peeled and sliced into matchstick pieces
2 tomatoes, skinned and sliced
½ cauliflower separated into small florets
3 shallots (or ½ small onion), finely chopped
4 fresh red chilies, finely chopped (or 4 dried chilies or 3 teaspoons chili powder)
½ cup shrimp, cooked and peeled
1 teaspoon salt
2 teaspoons caster sugar
3 tablespoons vinegar (white or malt)

Combine cucumber, carrot, tomatoes, cauliflower florets, shallots, and chilies with the shrimp, salt, sugar, and vinegar. Chill for at least one hour before serving.

SERVES 4.

ACAR KACANG

Peanut Pickle

4 fresh small green chilies (or 3 dried chilies or 2 teaspoons chili powder)

1 clove garlic

¼ cup roasted or fried peanuts

1 teaspoon soft brown sugar

Juice of 3 limes (or 2 lemons)

Salt and freshly ground black pepper to taste

Grind chilies and garlic in a mortar and pestle, or place in blender and mix. Crush peanuts and add (or add to blender).

Add the rest of the ingredients and mix; adjust seasoning with salt and pepper, and serve.

SERVES 4.

SERUNDENG

Coconut with Peanuts

Approximately 4 tablespoons vegetable oil for frying

6 shallots (or 1 medium onion), finely diced

3 cloves garlic, crushed

2 red chilies, very finely sliced into strips (or 2 dried chilies, or 1 teaspoon chili powder)

2 teaspoons ground coriander

1 cup coarsely grated or shredded coconut flesh (or dried coconut)

3 teaspoons dark brown sugar

Juice of 3 limes (or 1 large lemon)

Salt and freshly ground pepper to taste

½ cup water

¾ cup roasted peanuts

Heat the oil in a wok and add the shallots, garlic, chilies, and coriander, and fry for a few minutes. Add the coconut, sugar, lime juice, and seasoning, and continue to cook for about another 3 minutes. Stir in the water and continue cooking until the water has been absorbed.

Add the peanuts. Cover and continue to cook until the coconut is browned and slightly crispy. (If a very crispy dish is desired, broil or roast in a hot oven for 5 to 10 minutes before serving.) Allow to cool slightly before serving.

Serundeng will keep stored in an airtight container for up to 2 weeks.

SERVES 8.

SELADA DAN SAYUR

SALADS AND VEGETABLES

Indonesia is a treasure-trove of vegetables, many of which are still unknown in the West. Because the poorer members of Indonesian society cannot afford meat, much of the population exists on a simple but healthful vegetarian diet, made more substantial with the addition of tofu or tempeh.

Plants and flowers grow very quickly in the tropical heat, so people keep their gardens going everywhere; alongside railway tracks, and roads, etc. Anywhere you go, a host of vegetable plants and young papaya, coconut, and banana trees can be seen springing into life.

There are hundreds of imaginative ways in which vegetables are served. In the recipes below other vegetables can easily be substituted for the ones used.

The vegetable preparation time usually takes longer than the actual cooking, because the methods most often used are stir-frying, steaming, and parboiling.

GADO GADO
Vegetable Salad with a Spicy Peanut Sauce

This mixture of lightly cooked vegetables with a sauce poured over the top must be the one dish which is universally known as Indonesian. It can be served hot or cold and the peanut sauce, which is incredibly versatile, suits a host of other dishes, too. (See *Satay*, page 69, and *Lumpia Goreng*, page 60.)

> 1 small cauliflower
> 1 small cabbage

1 cup string beans

½ cup bean sprouts

3 medium-sized potatoes

3 medium-sized carrots

(other preferred vegetables can be used)

PEANUT SAUCE (use chilies according to how hot the sauce is preferred):

Approximately 6 tablespoons vegetable oil for frying

1 cup raw-skinned peanuts

2 cloves garlic

4 shallots (or 1 small onion)

Salt and freshly ground black pepper to taste

2 to 4 fresh red chilies (or 2 to 4 dried chilies, or 2 to 3 teaspoons chili powder)

1 teaspoon sugar

Approximately 2 cups water

2 tablespoons lime (or lemon) juice

1 hard-cooked egg, thinly sliced, to garnish or

4 shallots, thinly sliced and fried until crispy and golden brown

½ cucumber, peeled and sliced

Krupuk *(prawn crackers)*

Prepare the vegetables by cutting up the cauliflower into small florets, shredding the cabbage, slicing the beans, potatoes, and carrots, and rinsing the bean sprouts.

Prepare the sauce by frying the peanuts in approximately 4 tablespoons of the oil until crispy. Drain on paper towels and allow to cool. Grind them in a mortar and pestle or electric grinder.

Grind garlic, shallots, salt, and chilies in a mortar and pestle, or place in blender and mix until fairly smooth. Fry this paste in the remaining oil and then add the sugar.

Add the water and allow this mixture to come to a boil. Add the ground peanuts. Stir the mixture well and simmer until the sauce thickens.

Steam or boil the vegetables, starting with those which will need to cook the longest first (i.e., the potatoes followed by the carrots, then the cauliflower, beans, and cabbage. It is not really necessary to cook the bean sprouts at all). Make sure that the vegetables retain their crunchiness and their full color.

Heat up the peanut sauce when required and add the lime juice.

Arrange the vegetables as desired and pour the sauce over the top. (The vegetables are usually piled up on a large dish with the cabbage at the bottom and the garnishes placed on top before the sauce is poured over everything. They can alternatively be served in a large receptacle with separate sections with the sauce poured into the section in the middle.)

SERVES 4.

KAREDOK
Raw Vegetable Salad with a Spicy Peanut Dressing

This is similar to *Gado Gado* in that it is a vegetable salad with a peanut dressing, but the vegetables in this case are raw. The dressing is usually a little thinner and spicier and it is stirred into the vegetables rather than just being poured over the top.

This dish can be served by itself or with rice and meat dishes.

½ cup string beans
½ cup bean sprouts, cleaned
½ small white cabbage, cleaned
1 small head of lettuce, rinsed and drained
½ cucumber, rinsed, but preferably left unpeeled
Small bunch of fresh basil leaves, washed and torn into small pieces (untraditional, but they add a good bite to the dish)
2 tablespoons chopped fresh coriander or parsley leaves, to garnish

DRESSING:
½ cup raw peanuts
2 cloves garlic, crushed
1 slice terasi (optional)
½ -inch piece fresh ginger, crushed
5 small fresh green chilies (or 5 dried chilies, or 4 teaspoons chili powder)
A dash of salt and freshly ground black pepper
Approximately 1 cup boiling water
1 teaspoon sugar
2-inch piece tamarind soaked for 10 minutes in 4 tablespoons hot water and then squeezed and discarded to leave a colored juice (or 2 tablespoons lime or lemon juice)

Prepare vegetables: slice beans, finely shred cabbage and lettuce, slice cucumber. Mix with the basil leaves and bean sprouts.

Roast or fry the peanuts and then grind them in a mortar and pestle, or in an electric grinder.

Grind garlic, *terasi*, ginger, chilies, and salt and pepper in a mortar and pestle, or place in blender and mix until smooth. Pour on boiling water. Add sugar and tamarind water.

Add the ground peanuts to this mixture and then heat, stirring continuously for a few minutes. Leave to cool.

Arrange raw vegetables on plate. Stir in the dressing and sprinkle with the chopped coriander or parsley leaves.

SERVES 4.

URAP

Vegetable Salad with a Coconut Dressing

This is similar to the two preceding recipes in that it is made of a combination of vegetables which can either be cooked or left raw. The peanut dressing is replaced with a coconut sauce.

½ cup string beans, chopped
4 carrots, chopped
1 large green pepper, de-seeded and cut into strips
½ cucumber, left unpeeled and chopped
4 zucchini, left unpeeled and chopped

SAUCE:
3 cloves garlic, crushed
4 shallots (or 1 medium onion), roughly chopped
3 fresh green chilies (or 3 dried chilies, or 2 teaspoons chili powder)
¾ cup grated coconut flesh (or dried coconut)
½ cup water
1 teaspoon sugar
Salt and freshly ground pepper to taste

Prepare vegetables and leave raw or steam or parboil as desired.

Grind garlic, shallots, and chilies in a mortar and pestle, or place in blender and mix until smooth.

Put the coconut in a bowl and stir in the water, sugar, salt and pepper. Stir in the sauce.

Place bowl in a larger dish of water. Boil the water and steam the coconut for approximately 20 minutes.

Toss salad in dressing and serve.

SERVES 4.

ASINAN

Fruit and Vegetable Salad with a Sharp Dressing

This dish highlights the way in which Indonesian cuisine contrasts flavors and textures. It provides a good contrast to a chili-hot main course. It is very similar to *Rujak* (page 120).

> *1 small cabbage, cleaned and shredded*
> *½ cup bean sprouts, cleaned*
> *1 cucumber, chopped*
> *1 Chinese radish, chopped*
> *2 medium-sized apples, chopped*
> *1 bunch watercress, washed, drained, and chopped*
> *White vinegar (enough to cover and soak the above vegetables)*
>
> *DRESSING:*
> *¼ cup small dried shrimps, soaked briefly in hot water and drained (optional)*
> *2 red fresh chilies (or 2 dried chilies or 2 teaspoons chili powder)*
> *¼ cup fried peanuts*
> *2 tablespoons white vinegar*
> *A dash of salt and freshly ground black pepper*
> *1 cup dark brown sugar syrup, made by boiling sugar in approximately 1 cup water until syrupy, and then strained*

Soak all prepared vegetables in the vinegar for 2 hours.

In the meantime, prepare the dressing by grinding the shrimp, red chilies, and peanuts in a mortar and pestle, or place in a blender and mix until fairly smooth. Add the vinegar, salt, and sugar syrup, and stir well.

Drain the vegetables and allow to stand for 30 minutes, so the flavors mingle and mature and then pour the dressing over the vegetables.

SERVES 4.

LUMPIA GORENG
Stir-fried Vegetables Cooked in Pastry Wrappers

These small spring rolls are extremely popular as finger food at parties or as pre-dinner/lunch snacks; they are usually served hot with an accompanying peanut sauce (as for *Gado Gado* above), or a spicy chili sauce.

Any preferred vegetables can be used, but the bean sprouts should always be included. Small shrimp or cooked minced beef can also be used. Also, it is probably best to make a large batch and freeze any not immediately needed.

Approximately 3 tablespoons vegetable oil for frying plus enough to deep-fry the prepared rolls

6 shallots (or 1 large onion), finely diced

3 cloves garlic, crushed and finely chopped

2 small fresh green chilies, finely chopped (or 2 dried chilies or 1 teaspoon chili powder)

½-inch piece fresh ginger, crushed and finely chopped (or 1 teaspoon ground ginger)

½ small cabbage, cleaned and shredded

3 tablespoons dark soy sauce

1 teaspoon salt

3 carrots, chopped

¾ cup bean sprouts, rinsed and drained

¼ cup frozen peas

1 packet frozen pastry wrappers

Heat the oil in a wok. Fry the shallots, garlic, fresh chilies, and ginger for a few minutes. Add the carrots and cabbage and continue cooking for a few minutes, then add the soy sauce, salt, and bean sprouts.

Stir, turn off heat, and add the peas.

Lumpia are served quite small (usually about 3 inches in length by 1 inch in width), so if the packet of wrappers are large or square, you will need to divide them accordingly.

Place 1 tablespoon of filling onto the center of each wrapper, ensuring that there is not too much filling or the wrapper will burst during frying. Roll the wrapper around the filling, tucking in at the sides to secure.

Deep-fry until golden brown and drain on paper towels.

SERVES 4.

CAP CAI
Stir-fried Mixed Vegetables

This is a dish most clearly derived from the Chinese influence of lightly cooked vegetables which retain all of their color, texture, and flavor. It is a refreshing accompaniment to any spicy main course.

Indonesians often add shrimp or small pieces of offal, which can be added at the beginning of cooking if they are fresh, or at the end of cooking if they are already cooked and are being used up.

> *Approximately 4 tablespoons vegetable oil for frying*
> *2 cloves garlic, crushed*
> *4 shallots (or 1 small onion), roughly chopped*
> *1 stalk lemongrass, bruised (or 1 teaspoon grated lemon rind or ½ teaspoon powdered form)*
> *2 carrots, sliced*
> *1 small can bamboo shoots*
> *½ cup string beans, left whole if not too large*
> *½ small cabbage, cleaned and chopped*
> *4 sticks celery, chopped*
> *½ cup Chinese straw or black or ordinary button mushrooms, wiped and chopped*
> *Approximately ¼ cup beef stock or water*
> *2 tablespoons dark soy sauce*
> *Salt and freshly ground black pepper to taste*

Heat oil in wok. Add the garlic, shallots, and lemongrass. Stir fry the mixture for a few minutes only.

Add the vegetables (starting with the ones which take the longest to cook) and stir-fry until they are lightly cooked but still very crunchy and colorful.

Add the stock and stir for a minute. Add the soy sauce, salt and pepper to taste. Stir well, discard lemongrass and serve.

SERVES 4.

KANGKUNG
Stir-fried Greens

In the Sundanese restaurants in Jakarta, this dish is usually served bubbling and steaming on a hot plate.

SPICE PASTE:
8 shallots (or 2 medium-sized onions), roughly chopped
3 cloves garlic, crushed
5 fresh red chilies (or 5 dried chilies or 4 teaspoons chili powder)
3 candlenuts (or macadamia nuts or skinned almonds), crushed
2 tomatoes
Salt and freshly ground black pepper to taste
A dash of sugar

Approximately 3 tablespoons vegetable oil for frying
2 stalks lemongrass, bruised (or 1 teaspoon grated lemon rind or ½ teaspoon powdered form)
1 pound kangkung (water spinach is used in Indonesia, but any type of spinach, watercress, or greens is suitable for this dish), washed and chopped
½ cup water
8 pigeon eggs, or quail eggs, hard-cooked and shelled (optional)

Grind ingredients for spice paste in mortar and pestle, or place in blender and mix until smooth.

Heat the oil and fry the paste together with the lemongrass until fragrant. Add *kangkung* and stir-fry until limp.

Drain off excess oil and add water. Bring to a boil. Discard lemongrass and serve with the eggs whole.

SERVES 4.

Even favorite dishes are not immune to change. The one below was a popular favorite in one of the many Sundanese restaurants once situated around the rather monstrous *Monas* (National Monument) in the heart of Jakarta. Then suddenly, upon arrival in the area one evening, we thought we must have strayed into the wrong district: every one of the restaurants had been razed to the ground, apparently for no other reason than to provide more parkland space around the gigantic monument.

TUMIS TAUGE
Stir-fried Bean Sprouts with Tempeh

Approximately 3 tablespoons vegetable oil for frying

½ cup fresh or frozen tempeh (or fresh tofu if tempeh is unavailable)

2 large fresh red chilies, cut into very thin strips (or 2 dried chilies or 2 teaspoon chili powder)

1 cup bean sprouts, cleaned

Approximately ½ cup beef stock or water

2 tablespoons dark soy sauce

½ teaspoon dark brown sugar

Salt and freshly ground black pepper to taste

Heat oil in wok and add tempeh or tofu and stir-fry until crispy. Remove, drain on paper towels, and set aside.

Add chilies to the oil and cook for a few minutes. Add bean sprouts and stir-fry for one minute.

Add stock or water, and bring just to a boil. Add soy sauce and sugar. Adjust seasoning with salt and pepper, and serve.

SERVES 4.

KACANG BUNCIS DENGAN UDANG
String Beans Stir-fried with Shrimp

Approximately 3 tablespoons vegetable oil for frying

½ cup shrimp, cleaned, heads removed, de-veined and peeled

2 cloves garlic, crushed and finely chopped

1 cup string beans, left whole if not too large

Approximately ¾ cup beef stock or water

2 tablespoons dark soy sauce

Salt and freshly ground black pepper to taste

Heat oil in wok. Add shrimp and garlic and fry until the shrimp change color and the garlic begins to crisp a little.

Add beans and cook for 1 minute. Add stock (or water), and soy sauce. Cook for a few minutes until beans have softened a little but are still crunchy and retain their full color.

Adjust seasoning with salt and pepper, and serve.

SERVES 4.

SAMBAL GORENG KOL
Spicy Stir-fried Cabbage

Approximately 2 tablespoons vegetable oil for frying
6 shallots (or 1 medium onion), thinly sliced
3 fresh red chilies, crushed (or 3 dried chilies, or 3 teaspoons chili powder)
1 teaspoon dark brown sugar
1-inch piece fresh ginger, crushed and finely chopped (or 1 teaspoon ground ginger)
1 teaspoon salt
1 medium-sized cabbage, washed and coarsely chopped

Heat oil in wok and fry shallots until transparent. Add chilies, sugar, ginger, and salt. Stir-fry for 1 minute.

Add cabbage, stir, and cover. Simmer to soften the cabbage only slightly. Add a little water if mixture begins to burn.

Stir and serve.

SERVES 4.

TERUNG GORENG DENGAN BAWANG DAN CABE
Fried Eggplant with Shallots and Chilies

Eggplants in Indonesia are plentiful and make many popular dishes, but they are much smaller than those sold in the West.

2 medium-sized eggplants
2 tablespoons salt
Approximately 6 tablespoons vegetable oil for frying
6 shallots (or 1 medium onion), finely sliced
2 red chilies, finely sliced (or 2 dried chilies, or 2 teaspoons chili powder)
Salt and freshly ground black pepper to taste
1 tablespoon chopped coriander, or parsley leaves, to garnish

Slice the eggplants, sprinkle with salt, and leave to drain for approximately 20 minutes (to allow the bitterness to be extracted), then rinse and drain on paper towels.

Heat approximately 5 tablespoons of the oil in a wok and fry the eggplants, a few at a time, until they are cooked and crispy. Drain on paper towels.

In the remaining oil fry the shallots and chilies until crispy. Mix the eggplants, shallots, and chilies together. Adjust seasoning, adding salt and pepper, and garnish with the coriander, or parsley leaves.

Note: a moister dish can be obtained by simmering the shallots and chilies in ½ cup coconut milk (see Special Ingredients section) for 10 minutes (or until the milk thickens sufficiently), and then adding the fried eggplants.

SERVES 4.

ORAK ARIK JAGUNG MUDA
Stewed Baby Corn

Serve as an accompaniment to a meat or fish and rice dish.

4 shallots (or 1 small onion), finely diced
3 cloves garlic, crushed and finely chopped
½-inch piece fresh ginger, crushed and finely chopped (or 1 teaspoon ground ginger)
2 fresh red chilies, cut into very thin strips (or 2 dried chilies, or 2 teaspoons chili powder)
1 cup baby corn
Approximately ¾ cup coconut milk (see Special Ingredients section)

Place all ingredients in a wok. Bring mixture to a boil and then simmer until the coconut milk has been reduced and has thickened and the corn has softened but is still crunchy and retains its full color.

SERVES 4.

PEPES BUNGKUS
Mushrooms in a Parcel

SPICE PASTE:
10 fresh red chilies (or 10 dried chilies, or 5 teaspoons chili powder)
8 shallots (or 2 medium-sized onions) roughly chopped
5 candlenuts (or macadamia nuts or skinned almonds), crushed

2 tomatoes

1-inch piece ginger, crushed and chopped

1 teaspoon salt

1 teaspoon dark brown sugar

1 cup mushrooms (Chinese straw mushrooms are especially good, but button mushrooms
make a good substitute)

2 eggs, beaten

¾ cup coconut milk (see Special Ingredients section)

Aluminum foil (or banana leaves, if available)

Grind ingredients for spice paste in mortar and pestle, or place in blender and mix until smooth.

Wipe the mushrooms and slice thickly. Combine mushrooms with the eggs, coconut milk, and spice paste. Place in a large piece of foil and seal securely to make a packet. Steam (or bake if preferred) for approximately 25 minutes.

Carefully open the foil and empty into a serving dish.

SERVES 4.

AYAM, BEBEK, DAN TELUR
POULTRY AND EGGS

The Indonesian chicken, the so-called *ayam kampung* (village chicken), is what Westerners know as the bantam. *Ayam kampang* is a much leaner and smaller version of the bird bred in the West but authentic and successful dishes can still be produced using the Western variety.

Chickens roam everywhere in Indonesia, even in the streets of large cities. Health and animal-conscious people would be happy to hear that the chickens are "free range," but the rounding up in readiness for the cooking pot is totally unceremonious: groups of five or more can be tied together at the feet and sold in the markets (ducks are treated similarly), or twenty or more are crammed into rattan boxes and stacked up on lorries to be delivered to large restaurants. The most sorrowful sight of an Indonesian chicken is when a local ties up a group of birds and hangs them upside down on the handles of his motorbike as he drives through impossible traffic and noise!

Chicken is extremely important in Indonesian food. It is readily available and cheap and, unlike red meats, is essential to most traditional and ceremonial occasions. Duck is also very popular (especially on islands such as Bali) mainly because these birds can be reared in the wet paddies. The Indonesian duck is leaner and smaller version than in the West.

AYAM GORENG
Fried Chicken

8 chicken breasts, boned and skinned and each cut in half (any cuts of chicken can be used for this recipe)

1 stalk of lemongrass, bruised (or 1 teaspoon grated lemon rind or ½ teaspoon powdered form)

2½ cups coconut milk (see Special Ingredients section)

6 shallots (or 1 medium onion), finely diced

3 cloves garlic, crushed

8 candlenuts (or macadamia nuts or skinned almonds), crushed

1 teaspoon coriander seeds, crushed

1 fresh green chili, finely chopped (or 2 dried red chilies, or 1 teaspoon powdered chili)

1 teaspoon powdered turmeric

2 Kaffir lime leaves (or 1 bay leaf)

Salt and freshly ground black pepper to taste

Approximately 6 tablespoons vegetable oil for frying

Place all ingredients, except oil, in large saucepan and boil for approximately 20 minutes, or until chicken is tender and most of the juice has been absorbed.

Remove chicken and drain and discard the leftovers in the pan.

Heat the oil in a wok and fry the chicken pieces on both sides until they are golden brown.

Drain on paper towels and serve.

SERVES 4.

AYAM GORENG BUMBU
Spicy Fried Chicken

Ayam Goreng from the restaurant chain Nyonya Suharti is extremely popular in the large cities. The *Ayam Goreng* from this restaurant has a batter coating.

Follow the Fried Chicken recipe above for the chicken, then drain and put aside while making the batter.

COATING BATTER:
1½ cup rice flour (strong white flour will do)
2 teaspoons salt

A dash of freshly ground black pepper

½ teaspoon ground cumin

½ teaspoon coriander seeds, crushed

2 tablespoons melted butter

4 egg yolks, beaten

1 cup milk

2 egg whites, stiffly beaten

Enough vegetable oil to deep fry the chicken pieces

Sift the flour into a bowl with the salt. Mix in the black pepper, cumin, and coriander.

Mix the butter and egg yolks into the milk, and pour this onto the flour. Mix thoroughly and allow to stand for approximately 30 minutes.

Stir in stiffly beaten egg whites.

Coat the chicken pieces in the batter and fry in very hot oil until golden brown and crispy.

Drain on paper towels and serve.

SERVES 4.

SATAY AYAM
Chicken Kebabs

This dish is extremely common in Indonesia. Other meats are also used, but chicken is the most suitable. *Satay* is a specialty of the *warungs*, and it is always fascinating to watch the cooking process: the meat is cooked over hot charcoal in small terracotta receptacles and then it is furiously fanned by the owner of the stall, causing great wafts of aromatic and stifling smoke to grab the attention of passers-by. Small pieces of animal fat are often threaded in between the meat to add extra flavor and moisture, but this is not necessary unless desired.

Traditionally, *satay* is served on bamboo skewers (which should be soaked in water for about half an hour before the meat is threaded onto them), but metal skewers are just as good. This dish is ideal either as a snack, starter, main course with rice, or, perhaps most naturally, as part of a barbecue.

Satay of any type is generally served with the ubiquitous Indonesian peanut sauce. The recipe is given for *Gado Gado* on page 55.

4 chicken breasts, skinned and boned and cut up into ½-inch cubes
Skewers

MARINADE:
4 shallots (or 1 small onion), finely diced
6 tablespoons dark soy sauce
1 teaspoon dark brown sugar
2 tablespoons lime or lemon juice
1 small fresh green chili (or one dried chili), finely chopped

Mix the ingredients for the marinade. Soak the cubed chicken in the marinade for 1 to 2 hours in the refrigerator.

Thread the chicken onto the skewers and either broil or barbecue until tender but still firm.

Heat the peanut sauce and either serve separately or pour over the cooked satay.

SERVES 4.

GUDEG
Chicken and Jackfruit Casserole

This dish is from Yogyakarta in Central Java. Yogya, as it is affectionately known, is generally recognized as the cultural capital of Java and attracts thousands of artists and craftsmen. It abounds in theater and music and is a major university town. It is also a major batik producing center and daily hosts *wayang* puppet shows and *gamelan* recitals. In the surrounding area lie many temples and the magnificent Buddhist monument, Borobudur. In short, a visit to Yogya offers a glimpse of Indonesia's rich culture.

Despite all this activity, Yogya retains its laid-back and placid atmosphere. It is also a delight to be able to get about by *becak* (a hooded tricycle affair), which has now largely disappeared from big cities like Jakarta. The *becak* drivers are a strong, wiry, weatherbeaten crew, and will drive you around wherever you want to go. Transport via *becaks* makes for a very pleasant, leisurely, and even sleep-inducing experience, and adds a very special little something to the whole ambiance of the place. A Yogya *becak* ride is a world apart from sitting in the hideous traffic jams of Jakarta.

The dish below is, unlike most Indonesian dishes, inimitable, simply because *nanka* (jackfruit) is not readily available in the West. However, a similar dish can be created by using either fresh or canned mango or other firm fruit, or canned jackfruit.

SPICE PASTE:

8 shallots

3 cloves garlic

1 slice terasi *(or 2 teaspoons* balachan*) (optional)*

4 candlenuts (or macadamia nuts or skinned almonds), crushed

2 small fresh green chilies (or 2 dried chilies, or 2 teaspoons chili powder)

½-inch piece galingale (optional)

1 teaspoon ground cumin

3 teaspoons coriander seeds, crushed

1 small jackfruit, weighing approximately 1 pound (or equivalent weight of suggested alternatives)

2 Kaffir limes leaves (or 1 bay leaf)

Approximately 4 cups coconut milk (see Special Ingredients section)

1½ to 2 pounds cooked chicken pieces

A dash of salt and freshly ground black pepper

2 hard-cooked eggs, to garnish (optional)

1 tablespoon chopped coriander or parsley leaves, to garnish

Crush shallots, garlic, *terasi,* candlenuts, and chilies together into a paste, or place in blender and mix until smooth. Mix this paste with the galingale, cumin, and coriander.

Place all ingredients in a large wok. (If using a canned alternative to the jackfruit, do not add until 10 minutes before end of cooking.) Stir well, and season with a dash of salt and pepper.

Simmer until the sauce thickens (approximately 45 minutes), stirring occasionally to ensure that the chicken does not burn.

Discard the Kaffir lime leaves, garnish with the boiled eggs and coriander, or parsley leaves, and serve with plain boiled rice.

SERVES 4.

AYAM GURIH JAWA
Javanese Curried Chicken

Many expatriate families enjoy the best Indonesian food daily in their own homes, prepared by their Indonesian cooks. This is just one such popular dish.

Approximately 1 pound chicken cut into 1-inch cubes

3 teaspoons salt

Approximately 4 tablespoons vegetable oil for frying

8 shallots (or 1 large onion), chopped

4 cloves garlic, chopped

2 teaspoons ground turmeric

1 teaspoon coriander seeds, crushed

1 teaspoon ground cumin

1-inch piece grated ginger (or 1 teaspoon ground ginger)

1 stalk lemongrass, bruised (or ½ teaspoon powdered form)

2 fresh green chilies (or 2 dried chilies, or 2 teaspoons chili powder), crushed

1½ cups coconut milk (see Special Ingredients section)

Rub chicken with salt and fry in hot oil until golden brown.

Remove from pan and drain on paper towels.

Fry shallots and garlic for 2 minutes and then add turmeric, coriander, and cumin. Fry for 1 minute and then add the ginger, lemongrass, and chilies.

Return chicken to this mixture. Add coconut milk and cook uncovered until chicken is tender (approximately 30 to 40 minutes).

Discard lemongrass stalk before serving.

SERVES 4.

AYAM MASAK SANTEN
Chicken Cooked in Coconut Milk

This is a relatively mild dish.

1 teaspoon coriander seeds, crushed

1 teaspoon ground cumin

1 teaspoon freshly ground black pepper

½ teaspoon cloves, crushed

1 teaspoon ground turmeric

1 small green chili, chopped (or 1 dried chili or ½ teaspoon chili powder)

Approximately 4 tablespoons vegetable oil for frying

8 shallots (or 1 large onion), chopped

4 cloves garlic, crushed and chopped

1-inch piece of fresh ginger, crushed and finely chopped

2 pounds chicken meat, cut into bite-sized pieces

1 stalk lemongrass, bruised

2 Kaffir lime leaves (or 1 bay leaf)

Approximately 2 cups coconut milk (see Special Ingredients section)

2 tablespoons lime (or lemon) juice

Salt and freshly ground black pepper to taste

Combine all the spices, except the ginger, and mix using a little of the oil.

Heat the remaining oil in a wok and fry the shallots, garlic, and ginger until the shallots are transparent.

Add the spice mixture and chicken pieces and stir together until chicken is well coated and colored by the spice mixture. Add lemongrass, Kaffir lime leaves, and coconut milk and bring mixture to a gentle boil.

Simmer for 40 to 50 minutes until chicken is tender and the sauce is well thickened.

Add lime juice and adjust seasoning with salt and pepper.

Discard lemongrass and Kaffir lime leaves before serving.

SERVES 4.

SINGGANG AYAM
Baked Chicken

1 medium-sized chicken

Banana leaves (or aluminum foil)

Approximately 2 cups coconut milk (see Special Ingredients section)

2 teaspoons ground turmeric

2 Kaffir lime leaves (or 1 bay leaf)

1 stalk lemongrass, bruised (or 1 teaspoon lemon rind or ½ teaspoon powdered form)

2 tablespoons lime (or lemon) juice

SPICE PASTE:

10 small fresh green chilies (or 10 dried chilies), chopped

10 cloves garlic, crushed and roughly chopped

A dash of salt

Clean and quarter chicken.

Grease and line a baking dish with the banana leaves or foil and place chicken on top.

Grind ingredients for spice paste a in mortar and pestle, or place in blender and mix until smooth. Mix blended spice paste with coconut milk and pour into baking dish. Add turmeric, Kaffir lime leaves, lemongrass, and lime juice.

Cover the chicken pieces with more banana leaves or foil and cook in oven (400°F) for approximately 40 to 50 minutes, until the sauce has thickened.

Discard lemongrass and Kaffir lime leaves before serving.

SERVES 4.

AYAM GULUNG DADAR
Chicken Rolls

SPICE PASTE:

5 shallots (or 1 large onion)

2 cloves garlic, crushed and roughly chopped

½ teaspoon coriander seeds, crushed

½ teaspoon ground cumin

2 candlenuts (or macadamia nuts or skinned almonds), crushed

2-inch piece tamarind soaked in 4 tablespoons water for 10 minutes and then squeezed and discarded to leave a colored juice (or 1 tablespoon lime or lemon juice)

½ teaspoon dark brown sugar

A dash of salt and freshly ground black pepper

Approximately 1 pound boneless chicken breasts

¼ cup white flour

1 egg, beaten

½ cup coconut milk (see Special Ingredients section)

OMELETS:

3 eggs, beaten

½ teaspoon salt

½ teaspoon freshly ground black pepper

2 tablespoons water

1 tablespoon butter

Grind mixture for spice paste in mortar and pestle, or place in blender and mix until smooth.

Finely mince chicken and mix with flour, eggs, and spice mixture. Add coconut milk and mix until smooth, then set aside.

Mix all ingredients for omelets, except for the butter, and make 4 omelets.

Stack 2 omelets on top of each other. Spoon half the stuffing on top and neatly roll up the omelets. Repeat with other omelets.

Wrap up the omelets in waxed paper which has been greased with the butter. Fold and secure ends. Steam the rolls for approximately 30 minutes.

Unwrap the rolls and put them into a buttered baking tin and cook in the oven (400° F) until they are golden brown.

Remove and allow to cool. Cut into ½-inch thick slices.

Serve with a hot *sambal* and salad.

SERVES 4.

BEBEK BUNGKUS
Duck in a Parcel

There are many grumbles about how the island of Bali has been reduced from a paradise into a free-for-all tourist trap. Whatever the truth, Bali still remains a great "fun" place to visit. The largely Hindu population is peaceful and friendly, and the people generate a feeling that life is simply to be enjoyed.

Attractive traditional sights such as that of elegant women walking along in a procession with massive pots of offerings balanced delicately upon their heads are still seen, and the island is packed with temples and all sorts of dells and grottoes lying amid the spectacular countryside, where the steep hillsides are miraculously terraced.

Up in artistic Ubud, beautiful paintings and carvings can be bought and purchases can be reflected upon in one of the many excellent restaurants and cafes there, where anything from *Nasi Goreng* to carrot cake can be enjoyed.

Duck is relatively popular in Indonesia and especially in Bali. The dish given below is a traditional Balinese recipe.

1 oven-ready duck (approximately 3 to 3½ pounds)

MARINADE:
3 tablespoons lime (or lemon) juice

1 tablespoon sugar

1 teaspoon salt

1 teaspoon ground turmeric

1 large red chili, finely chopped (or 1 dried chili, or 1 teaspoon chili powder)

SPICE PASTE:

1 stalk lemongrass, bruised and chopped (or 1 teaspoon grated lemon rind, or 1 teaspoon
   powdered form)

4 fresh red chilies (or 4 dried chilies, or 3 teaspoons chili powder)

1½ tablespoons lime (or lemon) juice

1 teaspoon dark brown sugar

1 teaspoon salt

6 shallots (or 1 medium onion), roughly chopped

4 candlenuts (or macadamia nuts or skinned almonds), crushed

2 teaspoons freshly ground black pepper

Approximately 2 tablespoons vegetable oil for frying

Aluminum foil or banana leaves

2 scallions, chopped, to garnish

Combine marinade ingredients in a small bowl.

Place duck breast down in a large, deep dish. Cut deep diagonal slits all over the bird. Rub some of the marinade into the slits and all over the back. Turn the duck over.

Make more diagonal slits and work the marinade well into these incisions. Set aside for 1 hour.

Grind ingredients for spice paste in a mortar and pestle, or place in blender and mix until smooth.

Fry the spice paste in oil for about 10 minutes.

Pre-heat the oven to 350° F.

Spread out either a large piece of foil or banana leaves and place duck, breast down, in the center. Rub the spice mixture all over the bird and stuff the remaining mixture inside the duck. Fold the foil over the bird, crimping the edges together to prevent leakage of juices. Place the duck parcel on a baking tray and bake in a moderate oven for 1¾ hours.

Remove from oven and carefully open up the parcel. Pour out the collected liquid into a small pan and spoon off the fat. Heat this liquid gently.

Place the duck on a serving dish and spoon over the heated liquid. Garnish with the scallions.

SERVES 4.

BEBEK MASAK SANTEN
Duck Cooked in Coconut Milk

1 duck (approximately 3 to 3½ pounds) cooked and cut into serving pieces

SPICE PASTE:
6 shallots (or 1 onion), roughly chopped
3 cloves garlic, crushed and roughly chopped
2 candlenuts (or macadamia nuts or skinned almonds), crushed
1-inch piece fresh ginger (or 1 teaspoon ground ginger)
½ teaspoon ground or dried galingale (optional)
2 fresh small green chilies (or 2 dried chili, or 1 teaspoon chili powder)
Approximately 2 tablespoons vegetable oil for frying
2½ cups coconut milk (see Special Ingredients section)
A dash of salt and freshly ground black pepper
4 scallions, chopped, to garnish

Grind the ingredients for the spice mixture in a mortar and pestle, or place in blender and mix until smooth. Blend in 3 tablespoons of the coconut milk.

Place this mixture in a saucepan and bring to a boil and then add the duck pieces. Add remaining coconut milk and bring back to a boil.

Season and simmer for approximately 40 minutes. Serve garnished with scallions.

SERVES 4.

BEBEK PANGGANG
Broiled Duck

1 duck (approximately 3 to 3½ pounds), quartered
Approximately 3 tablespoons vegetable oil for frying
1 cup water

SPICE PASTE:

6 shallots (or 1 large onion), roughly chopped

4 cloves garlic, crushed and chopped

4 large red chilies, chopped (or 4 dried chilies, or 3 teaspoons chili powder)

1-inch piece fresh ginger, crushed and chopped (or 1 teaspoon ground ginger)

2 tomatoes

½ teaspoon dark brown sugar

A dash of salt and freshly ground black pepper

Grind ingredients for spice paste in mortar and pestle, or place in blender and mix until smooth.

Heat oil in wok and fry spice paste for a few minutes. Add duck and stir until totally covered in spice paste. Add water and continue cooking for about 15 minutes.

Remove and broil the duck over a medium heat while continuously brushing the meat with the sauce until the duck is golden brown.

Pour the remainder of the sauce over the duck and serve.

SERVES 4.

Eggs

Indonesians use duck eggs and other types, including the eggs we generally use in the West. Egg dishes are not abundant in Indonesian cooking, but eggs are generally present at most meals as a garnish: either shredded omelets are sprinkled over dishes or eggs are combined with the rice. At festivities, hard-cooked eggs are marbled with garish colors.

OMELET KEPITING
Crab Omelets

All sorts of ingredients are added to omelets in Indonesia, but this particular recipe was given to me by Ibu Soenario at The Oasis Restaurant and is prepared there in small batter molds.

6 eggs, beaten

1 carrot, peeled and finely diced

1 clove garlic, crushed and finely chopped

2 fresh small green chilies, finely chopped

3 scallions, finely chopped

¾ cup fresh crab meat (or 1 medium can)

A dash of salt and freshly ground black pepper

Mix together all ingredients.

Grease a tin of batter molds and cook in a moderate oven until done.

Alternatively, heat a little oil in a frying pan and cook in the normal way for omelets.

Serves 4.

SAYUR DENGAN TELUR
Vegetables Scrambled with Egg

Approximately 3 tablespoons vegetable oil for frying

6 shallots (or 1 medium onion), finely sliced

1 carrot, finely sliced

½ small white cabbage, finely shredded

1 zucchini, finely sliced

¼ cup bean sprouts

2 fresh red chilies, finely sliced lengthwise (or 2 dried chilies or 1 teaspoon chili powder)

A dash of salt and freshly ground pepper

3 large eggs, beaten

Heat the oil in a wok and fry the shallots for a few minutes.

Add the carrot for a few minutes and then add the cabbage, then the zucchini, and finally the bean sprouts.

Add the chilies and the seasoning and continue to cook for a few minutes. Stir in the beaten eggs and scramble with the vegetables. Serve immediately.

Serves 4.

TELUR DENGAN SAMBAL TOMAT CABE
Hard-Cooked Eggs with Chili Tomato Sauce

Approximately 2 tablespoons vegetable oil for frying

6 shallots (or 1 medium-sized onion), finely sliced

2 fresh red chilies, finely chopped (or 2 dried chilies or 1½ teaspoons chili powder)

6 tomatoes, skinned and roughly chopped (or 1 medium-sized can tomatoes)

1 teaspoon cloves, crushed

A dash of salt and freshly ground black pepper

Juice of 2 limes (or 1 lemon)

6 eggs, hard-cooked for 10 minutes

Heat the oil and fry the shallots until browned. Add the chilies, tomatoes, and cloves, and fry for a further 5 minutes. Add seasoning and lime juice.

Shell the eggs and halve and quarter them. Add to the sauce and continue to simmer for approximately 5 minutes.

SERVES 4.

IKAN DAN UDANG

FISH AND SHRIMP

As an archipelago surrounded by the Pacific and Indian Oceans and the Java and South China Seas, Indonesia naturally places a marked emphasis on fish and shellfish in its cuisine. Fish is an integral part of the diet and economy. Furthermore, because Indonesia depends on wet rice cultivation for a main staple food, the country is criss-crossed with paddies, reservoirs, and all sorts of irrigation systems, which in turn provide a wealth of freshwater fish and shrimp.

Down on the southwest coast of Java lies a little fishing town called Pelabuhan Ratu, just a three-hour drive from Jakarta. The daily catch is proudly laid out for the locals to choose from. The fresh fish can be eaten alfresco later on in the evening at the Bayu Amrta restaurant, situated high on a hill with an enviable view over the dramatic Indian Ocean, and a panoramic mountain backdrop.

Further down the coast at Pangumbahan, a very angry sea rages its surf toward a wild beach. In the evening, strange dark forms begin to emerge as female green turtles laboriously make their way to the top of the beach to lay their eggs. It's fascinating to observe these magnificent creatures making their monumental effort in order to perpetuate their species.

Once she has dug her nest with the slow, rhythmic movements of her front flippers, the female turtle lays her eggs at a rapid rate and then, just as carefully as she created the nest, she covers it all up and begins her long haul back down the beach to the sea. During the course of this move, she also stops frequently to dig out more mock nests. The whole process takes several hours. In the morning the beach resembles a sort of bizarre racetrack.

All too often, these beautiful creatures end up in big department stores in the cities, sold as trophies to adorn living room walls, etc. But in Pangumbahan, a special turtle reserve enables the turtles to have more of a chance of survival. Once the female turtle has returned to the sea, the eggs are dug up and placed in a little stockade until they hatch. The small turtles are then released into the sea after about a month, when they are strong enough to survive.

Indonesia has hundreds of fish species, many of which are generally be unknown in the West. However, excellent substitutes can be found and many dishes do use familiar fish such as red snapper, tuna, and pomfret.

Shrimp is the most popular and widely used shellfish. It is used in many things, even *krupuk* (prawn crackers) and *terasi (balachan)*. If possible, it is better to use fresh shrimp, but frozen will do. Shrimp not to be left in the shell should be de-veined.

In Indonesia fish and shellfish are usually sold live. All the following recipes, unless specified, begin with cleaned fish quantities (the head and guts have been removed, the skin has been de-scaled and the fish has been thoroughly rinsed in cold running water).

IKAN PANGGANG
Whole Broiled Sour and Spicy Fish

Approximately 2 pounds fish (either 1 large fish or 2 small fish) such as pomfret, sole, or turbot
½ teaspoon salt
2 tablespoons lime (or lemon) juice

SPICE PASTE:
1-inch piece ginger, crushed and chopped (or 1 teaspoon ground ginger)
½-inch piece galingale (or 1 teaspoon dried or powdered form)
1 stalk lemongrass, bruised (or 1 teaspoon grated lemon rind or ½ teaspoon powdered form)
4 fresh red chilies, chopped (or 3 dried chilies, or 2 teaspoons chili powder)
6 shallots (or 1 large onion), peeled and roughly chopped
4 cloves garlic, crushed and roughly chopped
1 teaspoon ground turmeric
½ teaspoon salt
3 tablespoons lime (or lemon) juice

1 cup coconut milk (see Special Ingredients section)
A little vegetable oil to brush broiling pan
Lime (or lemon) wedges to garnish

Make three or four diagonal slits across both sides of the fish. Rub in the salt and the 2 tablespoons lime juice over the whole of the fish. Set aside for 20 to 30 minutes.

Grind ingredients for the spice paste in a mortar and pestle, or place in blender and mix until smooth.

Spread the spice paste into a shallow ovenproof dish large enough to hold the fish. Mix in the coconut milk. Place the fish in the dish and spoon over some of the marinade. Set aside for about 10 minutes and baste from time to time.

Pre-heat broiler and brush the rack lightly with oil. Remove fish from the marinade and place on the rack. Cook for 20 to 30 minutes or until the fish has cooked through. Baste fish frequently and generously with marinade and turn the fish every 5 minutes.

Finish basting 5 minutes before end of cooking to allow the spice paste to form a crust. Garnish with lime wedges.

SERVES 4.

IKAN UJUNG KULON
Fish Ujung Kulon

In recent years Indonesia has come under escalating world pressure to curb the depletion of its natural resources and animal species.

The nature reserve of Ujung Kulon, situated on the southwestern tip of Java, represents just one of the attempts to meet this demand. It is the final home of the Javanese rhino, which has been hunted to the brink of extinction. Only an estimated sixty rhino are left, all living at Ujung Kulon.

The reserve itself provides a haven of fauna and flora for the hundreds of other animal and fish species that inhabit it. Visitors can stay on the tiny islands of Peucang and Handeleum, (where Ujung Kulon is located) to enjoy the idyllic peace of this place.

This recipe originates from the small restaurant on Peucang Island, headed by Chef Hartoyo, which caters to occasional tourists and fishermen. Meals are eaten outside to the accompaniment of insect sounds and the wonderful sights of the reserve. The gracious and prehistoric-looking hornbills inspire amazement at the energy and slightly ghostly sound produced by their wings as they fly overhead. Deer timidly graze in the dying light as the fishermen bring in their catch of various fish, and the resident monkeys see what pranks they can get up to and what chaos they can cause.

Approximately 1½ pounds fish fillets (red snapper or cod)
4 tablespoons malt vinegar
½ teaspoon salt
Approximately 6 tablespoons vegetable oil for frying
4 cloves garlic, crushed and chopped
2-inch piece ginger, crushed and cut into matchstick pieces
3 fresh red chilies, finely chopped (or 3 dried chilies or 2 teaspoons chili powder)
6 carrots, peeled and cut into small, thin matchsticks
4 tablespoons tomato paste
1 cup water
2 tablespoons lime (or lemon) juice
1 teaspoon dark brown sugar
3 eggs, beaten
¾ cup white flour
3 scallions, chopped, to garnish
A dash of salt and freshly ground black pepper

Cut fillets into 1- to 2-inch pieces.

Rub 2 tablespoons vinegar and ½ teaspoon salt into the fish and set aside for a little while.

Heat a little of the oil in a wok and fry the garlic and ginger. Add the chilies and carrots and continue to fry for a few minutes.

Drain off excessive oil and add the tomato paste and water and simmer for 1 minute. Add the lime juice, remaining vinegar, and sugar. Keep this sauce warm.

Drain fish and dip the pieces into the beaten eggs and then the flour.

Heat remaining oil in a wok and fry the fish until golden and crispy. Arrange fish on a platter and cover with the sauce. Garnish with the scallions.

SERVES 4.

IKAN GURAME DI GORENG KERING
Crispy-fried Pomfret

BATTER:

¾ *cup rice (or strong white) flour*

1 teaspoon salt

1 tablespoon melted butter

2 egg yolks, beaten

½ *cup milk*

1 egg white, stiffly beaten

2 pomfret (or similar) fish, each weighing approximately 1 pound each, cleaned but with heads still intact

2 teaspoons salt

Enough vegetable oil to deep-fry the fish

Make the batter by sifting the flour into a bowl with the salt. Mix the butter and egg yolks into the milk and pour this onto the flour. Mix thoroughly and allow to stand for 30 minutes. Then stir in stiffly beaten egg white.

Prepare the fish by making a long slit on the underside, parallel to the backbone. Rub in salt and then coat with the batter, ensuring that the inside of the slit is thoroughly covered.

Heat oil in wok and fry fish until crispy golden brown on outside and tender on the inside. Drain on paper towels.

Serve with plain rice and a hot *sambal*.

SERVES 4.

GULAI IKAN
Fish Curry

2 cups coconut milk (see Special Ingredients section)

1½ pounds firm white fish (red snapper, cod, turbot)

A dash of salt and freshly ground black pepper

SPICE PASTE:

10 shallots (or 2 large onions), roughly chopped

3 cloves garlic, crushed and chopped

1 teaspoon coriander seeds, crushed

1 teaspoon ground cumin

1 teaspoon ground turmeric

1 teaspoon dark brown sugar

4 fresh red chilies (or 4 dried chilies, or 3 teaspoons chili powder)

*2-inch piece tamarind soaked for 10 minutes in 4 tablespoons hot water, then squeezed
and discarded to leave colored juice (or 4 tablespoons lime or lemon juice)*

Approximately 2 tablespoons vegetable oil for frying

Prepare coconut milk.

Chop fish into bite-sized pieces and season with salt and pepper.

Grind ingredients for spice paste in a mortar and pestle, or place in blender and mix until smooth. Stir in tamarind juice.

Fry the paste in oil for a few minutes. Add the fish and coconut milk and simmer gently for 7 to 10 minutes or until cooked, but do not boil. Adjust seasoning with salt and pepper and serve with plain rice.

SERVES 4.

IKAN KECAP

Fish in Soy Sauce

2 tablespoons vegetable oil for frying

8 shallots (or 1 large onion), finely chopped

3 cloves garlic, crushed and chopped

4 fresh green chilies (or 4 dried chilies, or 2 teaspoons chili powder)

*1 stalk lemongrass, bruised and chopped (or 1 teaspoon grated lemon rind or ½ teaspoon
powdered form)*

Approximately 2 pounds fish fillets cut into thick slices

3 tablespoons dark soy sauce

1 teaspoon dark brown sugar

3 tablespoons lime (or lemon) juice

1 teaspoon freshly grated nutmeg (or 1 teaspoon ground nutmeg)

1 clove, crushed

2 Kaffir lime leaves (or 1 bay leaf)

1 cup water

Salt and freshly ground black pepper to taste

Heat the oil in a wok and add shallots, garlic, chilies, and lemon grass. Stir-fry until the onions are transparent. Add the fish and fry on both sides for a few minutes. Add the soy sauce, sugar, lime juice, nutmeg, clove, and Kaffir lime leaves and fry for a few more minutes.

Pour in the water and adjust seasoning with salt and pepper. Simmer until the fish is tender (approximately 10 minutes).

Discard the lemongrass and the Kaffir lime leaves before serving.

SERVES 4.

IKAN BUMBU PEDAS
Spiced Fish in a Hot Sauce

Approximately 2 pounds firm white fish

2 teaspoons ground turmeric mixed with a little water to form a paste

1 teaspoon salt

2 tablespoons lime (or lemon) juice

Approximately 6 tablespoons vegetable oil for frying

1 stalk lemongrass, bruised (or 1 teaspoon grated lemon rind or ½ teaspoon powdered form)

1 cup water

3 tablespoons dark soy sauce

SPICE PASTE:

6 fresh chilies, chopped (or 6 dried chilies, or 4 teaspoons chili powder)

10 shallots (or 1 large onion), roughly chopped

5 cloves garlic, crushed and chopped

5 candlenuts (or macadamia nuts or skinned almonds), crushed

1-inch piece ginger, crushed and chopped (or 1 teaspoon ground ginger)

2-inch piece tamarind soaked for 10 minutes in 4 tablespoons hot water, and then squeezed and discarded to leave a colored juice (or 1 tablespoon lime or lemon juice)

Salt and sugar, to taste

Cut fish into slices. Rub with turmeric paste, salt, and lime juice. Allow to stand for 10 minutes.

Heat the oil in a wok and add the fish and fry until golden brown. Drain and set aside.

Grind ingredients for spice paste in mortar and pestle, or place in blender until smooth and then fry for a few minutes. Add lemongrass, water, and soy sauce.

When mixture has come to a boil, add the fried fish. Stir and simmer until the sauce has thickened. Discard lemongrass before serving, and skim off any excess oil.

SERVES 4.

GULAI UDANG
Shrimp Curry

2 cups medium-to large-sized shrimp
2 ripe tomatoes, sliced
1 stalk lemongrass, bruised (or 1 teaspoon grated lemon rind or ½ teaspoon powdered form)
2 Kaffir lime leaves (or 1 bay leaf)

SPICE PASTE:
10 shallots (or 1 large onion), roughly chopped
4 cloves garlic, crushed and chopped
1-inch piece ginger, crushed and chopped
8 fresh red chilies, crushed (or 8 dried chilies, or 4 teaspoons chili powder)
1 teaspoon ground turmeric
½ teaspoon salt

4 cups coconut milk (see Special Ingredients section)

Clean shrimp and remove heads but do not peel them.

Grind ingredients for spice paste in mortar and pestle, or place in blender and mix until fairly smooth. Stir the paste into the coconut milk and then add the lemongrass and Kaffir lime leaves.

Bring mixture to a boil in a wok, stirring continuously. Add the shrimp and tomatoes and cook for approximately 7 minutes or until prawns are cooked through. Discard lemongrass and Kaffir lime leaves and serve with plain boiled rice, a salad, and a hot *sambal.*

SERVES 4.

UDANG GORENG ASAM MANIS

Sweet and Sour Jumbo Shrimp

12 large fresh Jumbo Shrimp (if possible; if not, frozen will do, or 1 pound of fish filets
*   can be used if preferred)*

1 teaspoon salt

1 egg, lightly beaten

2 tablespoons white flour

Enough vegetable oil to deep-fry the jumbo shrimp

SWEET AND SOUR SAUCE:

2 tablespoons dark soy sauce

1 tablespoon tomato paste

4 tablespoons malt vinegar

4 tablespoon sugar

2 teaspoons cornstarch mixed with 4 tablespoons water

½ cup water

Shell and de-vein jumbo shrimp and rub with salt.

Mix egg and flour. Place shrimp in this mixture and coat well.

Deep fry in very hot oil until golden brown. Remove and drain on paper towels.

To make the sauce, combine all sauce ingredients, bring to the boil and pour over the fried prawns.

SERVES 4.

SAMBAL GORENG UDANG

Fried Jumbo Shrimp in Spicy Coconut Milk

SPICE PASTE:

4 shallots (or 1 small onion), roughly chopped

3 cloves garlic, crushed and chopped

2 fresh red chilies, chopped (or 2 dried chilies, or 2 teaspoons chili powder)

1-inch piece ginger, crushed and chopped

1 teaspoon coriander seeds, crushed

1 tablespoon vegetable oil for frying

2 cups jumbo shrimp, shelled and de-veined

1 cup coconut milk (see Special Ingredients section)

A dash of salt and freshly ground black pepper

Grind ingredients for spice paste in mortar and pestle, or place in blender and mix until smooth.

Heat oil in wok and add the paste. Gently fry and stir the mixture until browned.

Add the jumbo shrimp and coat them with the paste. Add the coconut milk, and season with salt and pepper.

Stir and boil very gently until the shrimp are tender and the sauce has thickened. Adjust seasoning with more salt and pepper if required.

SERVES 4.

UDANG MASAK NANAS
Shrimp Cooked with Pineapple

1½ cups medium-sized shrimp

3 tablespoons vegetable oil for frying

4 cloves garlic, crushed and chopped

4 fresh red chilies, cut into 1-inch slices (or 4 dried chilies, or 3 teaspoons chili powder)

½ cup coconut milk (see Special Ingredients section)

1 small fresh pineapple, chopped (or 1 large can pineapple chunks, drained)

1 clove, crushed

A dash of sugar, malt vinegar and salt, to taste

1 tablespoon chopped dill, to garnish

Clean the shrimp and remove the heads, but do not peel them.

Heat the oil in a wok and stir-fry the garlic and chilies for a few minutes. Add the shrimp. Add the coconut milk, pineapple, clove, sugar, salt, and vinegar. Cook for approximately 5 minutes, or until done. Remove and serve.

SERVES 4.

UDANG GORENG DENGAN LIQUOR
Fried Shrimp with Sherry

Westerners often feel squeamish when they observe how Asians sometimes behave in relation to animals.

Many restaurants in Indonesia serve a variation of this dish, called *Udang Mabok*, literally, "Drunken Shrimp". The waiter comes to the table with a dishful (usually a glass, so that the spectacle may be fully observed) of live shrimp. He pours some alcohol over the poor things, covers the dish and shakes it vigorously. He then places the dish over a flame to cook the by-now comatose contents.

1½ cups medium-sized shrimp
3 tablespoons vegetable oil for frying
2 cloves garlic, crushed and chopped
5 fresh red chilies, cut into 1-inch slices (or 5 dried chilies, or 3 teaspoons chili powder)
¾ cup sherry (or other desired alcohol)

Clean the shrimp and remove the heads, but do not peel them.

Heat the oil in a wok and stir-fry the garlic and chilies for a few minutes. Add the shrimp and stir-fry for a minute.

Add sherry. Cover and simmer for a few minutes until tender.

SERVES 4.

UDANG BAKAR
Whole Broiled Jumbo Shrimp

This dish is extremely simple but very refreshing and tasty. It makes an excellent starter served on large leaves of lettuce and garnished with tomato and wedges of lime (or lemon).

8 large Jumbo Shrimp

MARINADE:
2 tablespoons lime (or lemon) juice
4 tablespoons dark soy sauce
3 cloves garlic, crushed and chopped
3 small green chilies, crushed and chopped (or 3 dried chilies, or 2 teaspoons chili powder)
A dash of sugar, salt, and vinegar, to taste
A little oil or melted butter

Mix together ingredients for marinade.

Clean the jumbo shrimp and partly shell them, but keep the heads and tails intact. Slice them lengthwise down the middle to open them out flat. Leave them to soak in the marinade for about an hour.

Broil them on oiled or buttered aluminum foil for 6 to 10 minutes, turning them frequently and brushing with the remaining marinade.

SERVES 4.

UDANG REBUS

Steamed Shrimp

Shrimp are often steamed with the popular *Pete* bean which grows in Indonesia. The beans grow in large pods and have a slightly nutty and bitter flavor. They are available in cans, but a variation on the recipe below, *Udang Pete Rebus*, can be created by using broad beans added just before the shrimp are steamed.

> *1½ cups medium-sized shrimp*
>
> *MARINADE:*
> *3 tablespoons dark soy sauce*
> *3 cloves garlic, crushed and chopped*
> *1-inch piece ginger, crushed and chopped*
> *4 fresh green chilies, chopped (or 4 dried chilies, or 3 teaspoons chili powder)*
> *2 tablespoons lime (or lemon) juice*
> *1 teaspoon dark brown sugar*

Clean shrimp and remove heads, but do not peel them.

Mix together ingredients for marinade. Leave shrimp to soak in marinade for about 1 hour.

Steam in a covered colander for about 6 minutes or until tender and fragrant.

SERVES 4.

BAKWAN

Shrimp and Bean Sprout Fritters
¾ cup white flour
¼ teaspoon baking soda
1 teaspoon ground ginger
1 teaspoon ground coriander
2 red chilies, finely chopped (or 2 dried chilies, or 1 teaspoon chili powder)

A dash of salt and freshly ground black pepper

4 eggs, beaten

½ cup water

¾ cup shrimp, cleaned and peeled

2 shallots (or ½ small onion)

½ cup bean sprouts

4 scallions, chopped

Enough vegetable oil to deep-fry in a wok

Sift the flour with the baking soda. Add ginger, coriander, chilies, and salt and pepper. Add the eggs and then the water, stirring continuously to ensure that the mixture does not become lumpy.

Finely chop or mince the shrimp and shallots and add to mixture. Clean bean sprouts and scallions and add to mixture.

Heat the oil in a wok. Plunge a soup ladle into the hot oil for a second. Remove and fill it with a spoonful of the batter.

Dip the ladle into the hot oil and let it stay there until the fritter floats free.

Continue frying until fritters are golden brown. Serve hot or cold.

SERVES 4.

DAGING

MEAT

In Indonesia meat dishes are not as important as vegetable and fish dishes, partly because meat is more expensive and also because there is such an abundance of other foods available. When meat is used, however, it is usually cut up into very small pieces and combined with many other ingredients. This method makes for substantial but not heavy dishes.

Indonesians do not place much emphasis on the specific cuts of meat nor on the type of meat to be used: beef is often really water buffalo, lamb is often goat, and so on. The Batak people of Menado are known to eat dog, and even human flesh— known as "long pig"—was consumed in Irian Jaya until very recently.

RENDANG DAGING SAPI
Beef Cooked in Coconut Milk

This Western Sumatra dish is probably one of the only ones which uses large chunks of beef (or more traditionally, water buffalo), combined with spices and coconut milk.

Because water buffalo was traditionally the main ingredient, cooking time was very long in order to tenderize the meat. When all the sauce had been reduced and dried up, the resulting dish had excellent preservative qualities and could be kept for a good length of time; it was often known as "traveler's food."

A western taste would likely appreciate the beautiful sauce in which the meat is cooked. A similar dish, *Kaliyo* (exactly the same ingredients, but the meat isn't cooked for quite so long so that more sauce is left) may be preferable.

SPICE PASTE:

2 teaspoons salt

20 shallots (or 3 large onions), roughly chopped

6 cloves garlic, crushed and chopped

3 teaspoons ground turmeric

2-inch piece fresh ginger, crushed and chopped

10 fresh red chilies, chopped (or 10 dried chilies or 5 teaspoons chili powder)

2 kemiri nuts (or macadamia nuts or skinned almonds), crushed (optional)

½ teaspoon powdered galingale (optional)

2 pounds stewing steak, cubed

6 to 8 cups coconut milk (see Special Ingredients section)

2 stalks lemongrass, bruised (substitutes not really suitable for this dish)

3 Kaffir lime leaves (or 2 bay leaves)

Grind the ingredients for the spice paste in a mortar and pestle, or place in blender and mix until fairly smooth.

Mix the beef with the spice paste and the coconut milk in a large wok and add the lemongrass and the Kaffir lime leaves. Stir occasionally and bring the mixture to a boil and cook until the coconut milk has thickened (approximately 1½ hours). Reduce the heat and cook until the oil is separated and can be skimmed.

This should take around another hour for *Kaliyo.* If the drier *Rendang* is desired, continue simmering, and occasionally stirring, for a further 30 to 50 minutes.

Discard the lemongrass and Kaffir lime leaves, adjust seasoning with extra salt, and serve with a green salad, plain rice, and a *sambal.*

SERVES 4.

DENDENG RAGI
Sliced Beef with Grated Coconut

SPICE PASTE:

8 shallots (or 1 medium onion), roughly chopped

4 cloves garlic, crushed and chopped

1 tablespoon coriander seeds, crushed

A dash of salt

2 tablespoons dark brown sugar

1-inch piece tamarind soaked for 10 minutes in 2 tablespoons water then squeezed and discarded to leave a colored juice (or 2 tablespoons lime or lemon juice)

1 coconut (or approximately 1 cup dried coconut)

2 pounds lean beef (such as filet)

1 stalk lemongrass, bruised (or 1 teaspoon grated lemon rind, or ½ teaspoon powdered form)

1-inch piece ginger, crushed and chopped

2 Kaffir lime leaves (or 1 bay leaf)

1 cup water

2 tablespoons vegetable oil

½ cup fried peanuts

Grind spice mixture in mortar and pestle, or place in blender and mix until smooth.

Coarsely grate the coconut.

Slice the beef into thin 3 inch by 3½ inch squares.

Mix the grated coconut, beef, spice paste, lemongrass, ginger, and Kaffir lime leaves in a wok. Add the water and simmer the mixture stirring occasionally. When the water has been boiled away, add the oil and fry the mixture until the meat and coconut are golden brown and dry. Drain off any excess oil.

Add the peanuts and stir until well blended. Discard lemongrass and Kaffir lime leaves before serving.

SERVES 4.

EMPAL

Spicy Fried Slices of Beef

1 pound lean beef (such as filet)

1 cup water

Approximately 5 tablespoons vegetable oil for frying

SPICE PASTE:

1 teaspoon coriander seeds, crushed

4 cloves garlic, crushed and chopped

1-inch piece ginger, crushed and chopped

½ teaspoon salt

A dash of sugar

1-inch piece tamarind soaked for 10 minutes in 2 tablespoons water and then squeezed and discarded to leave a colored juice (or 1 tablespoon lime or lemon juice)

Cook the beef in the water until tender. Remove and set aside half the water.

Cut the beef into 3 inch by 3 inch squares, of ½-inch thickness. Pound and flatten each piece of beef slightly in order to tenderize as much as possible.

Grind ingredients for spice paste in a mortar and pestle, or place in blender and mix until smooth. Stir the paste into the water which has been put aside. Add the slices of beef and allow to marinate for about 20 minutes.

Heat oil in wok and add beef. Fry until the beef is brown and crisp.

SERVES 4.

CABE ISI

Stuffed Chili Peppers

½ pound cooked minced beef filet
4 medium-sized potatoes, boiled and mashed
Enough vegetable oil to shallow-fry the chili peppers
2 eggs
16 large green or red chilies

SPICE PASTE:
1 teaspoon coriander seeds, crushed
6 shallots (or 1 medium onion) roughly chopped
4 cloves garlic, crushed and chopped
A dash of salt and freshly ground black pepper

Mix the potatoes with the beef.

Grind ingredients for spice paste in a mortar and pestle, or place in blender and mix until smooth. Add the paste to the beef and potatoes. Beat one of the eggs and stir into the beef and potato mixture.

Make a slit throughout the length of each of the chilies, but do not cut right through them. De-seed, wash, and drain the chilies.

Beat the other egg and brush the inside of the chilies. Stuff the chili peppers with the meat and potato mixture. Brush the remaining egg on the outside of the chilies.

Heat the oil in a wok and fry for approximately 10-15 minutes or until the chilies are thoroughly cooked through.

SERVES 4.

MARTABAK
Beef-stuffed Savory Pancakes

This is a very popular *warung* dish in Indonesia, and it is fascinating to watch the stall holder's expertise and swiftness in preparing these substantial snacks.

The stall holder will roll out his pastry until it is paper thin. This is very difficult to copy, but it does not matter as it is easier to use pre-prepared pastry anyway.

12 shallots (or 2 large onions), finely sliced
3 cloves garlic, peeled and crushed
Approximately 4 tablespoons vegetable oil
1 teaspoon coriander seeds, finely crushed
1 teaspoon ground cumin
1-inch piece ginger, crushed and chopped (or 2 teaspoons ground ginger)
2 small chilies, chopped (or 1 teaspoon chili powder)
1 teaspoon ground turmeric
1 pound minced beef filet
5 scallions, chopped
3 eggs
1 packet wonton sheets (widely available in Chinese grocery stores)
Enough vegetable oil to shallow-fry the martabak

Heat the 3 tablespoons of oil in a wok and fry the shallots and garlic until soft. Add coriander, cumin, ginger, chili, and turmeric and mix thoroughly. Fry for 1 more minute and then add the minced beef and cook for 15 more minutes.

Allow to cool and then empty the meat mixture into a bowl and add the scallions.

Beat the eggs and add to the bowl.

Lay half the wonton skins onto a board and place 1 to 2 tablespoons of the meat mixture onto each skin. Top with another skin, dampen the edges with a little water and seal together.

Heat the oil for frying the prepared pancakes in a wok until very hot and fry for approximately 3 to 4 minutes on each side, turning once. Drain on paper towels and serve hot.

Can be decorated with small fresh red and green whole chilies.

SERVES 4.

PERKEDEL DAGING
Meatballs in Coconut Milk

1 pound minced beef filet
A dash of salt
1 egg, beaten
Approximately 5 tablespoons vegetable oil for frying
6 fresh red chilies, sliced (or 6 dried chilies or 4 teaspoons chili powder)
2 Kaffir lime leaves (or 1 bay leaf)
1-inch piece ginger, crushed and chopped
1 cup shrimp, de-veined, heads removed, and rinsed
1 teaspoon dark brown sugar
2 cups coconut milk (see Special Ingredients section)

SPICE PASTE:
10 shallots (or 2 medium onions), roughly chopped
4 cloves garlic, crushed and chopped
10 fresh red chilies (or 10 dried chilies or 6 teaspoons chili powder)

Combine beef with the salt and beaten egg. Shape into meatballs of desired size.

Heat 3 tablespoons of the oil in a wok and fry the meatballs until dark brown. Drain and set aside.

Grind the ingredients for the spice paste in a mortar and pestle, or place in blender and mix until smooth.

Heat the remaining oil in a wok and fry the spice paste, chilies, Kaffir lime leaves, and ginger for about 5 minutes.

Add shrimp and sugar. Add the meatballs and coconut milk when the shrimp have changed color. Cook until the coconut milk has evaporated, stirring occasionally. Remove Kaffir lime leaves before serving.

SERVES 4.

GULAI KAMBING
Spicy Lamb or Mutton Curry

½ cup freshly grated coconut (or dried coconut)

SPICE PASTE:

2 teaspoon coriander seeds, crushed

1 teaspoon ground cumin

1 teaspoon freshly grated nutmeg (or 1 teaspoon ground nutmeg)

1 teaspoon ground turmeric

6 small fresh green chilies (or 6 dried chilies, or 4 teaspoons chili powder)

4 cloves garlic, crushed and chopped

1-inch piece ginger, crushed and chopped

Approximately 4 tablespoons vegetable oil for frying

12 shallots (or 2 medium onions), chopped

1-inch piece cinnamon stick

2 cloves

2 pounds lean lamb or mutton, chopped into 1-inch cubes

3 cups coconut milk (see Special Ingredients section)

Salt and freshly ground black pepper to taste

Dry fry the coconut in a wok until it is lightly browned (alternatively, broil it) and set aside.

Grind the ingredients for the spice paste in a mortar and pestle, or place in blender and mix until smooth.

Heat the oil in a wok and fry the shallots until transparent. Add the spice paste, cinnamon stick, and cloves, and stir-fry for a few minutes. Discard the cinnamon and cloves.

Stir in the dry-fried coconut, and the meat. Cook and stir the mixture over a moderate heat until the meat is browned on all sides.

Add the coconut milk and bring the mixture slowly to a boil, stirring constantly. Reduce the heat and simmer, stirring occasionally, until the meat is tender (approximately 1 hour for lamb and longer for mutton).

SERVES 4.

KAMBING ASAM PEDAS
Hot and Sour Lamb

1½ pounds lean lamb

1 teaspoon salt

SPICE PASTE:

8 shallots (or 1 large onion)

3 cloves garlic

1-inch piece ginger, crushed and chopped

2-inch piece tamarind soaked for 10 minutes in 4 tablespoons hot water and then squeezed and discarded to leave a colored juice (or 2 tablespoons lime or lemon juice)

1 teaspoon coriander seeds, crushed

4 fresh chilies (or 4 dried chilies, or 3 teaspoons chili powder)

Approximately 6 tablespoons vegetable oil for frying

6 tomatoes, sliced

½ cup hot water

Salt and freshly ground black pepper to taste

Slice the meat thinly, and then into bite-sized pieces. Place in bowl and rub with the salt and set aside in a cool place.

Grind the ingredients for the spice paste in a mortar and pestle, or place in blender and mix until smooth.

Heat 4 tablespoons of the oil in a wok and fry meat for 3 minutes (you may have to do this in batches). Remove and drain on paper towels.

Fry the spice paste in the remaining oil, stirring continuously.

Replace the meat and continue stirring for 2 minutes, then add the tomatoes and hot water. Stir well and cook for a further few minutes. Adjust seasoning with salt and pepper to taste. Serve with plain rice.

SERVES 4.

In a little town called Gianyar to the northeast of Bali's capital Denpasar, *Babi Guling* (Suckling Pig) is a celebrated dish. Upon the recommendation of some friends, we made our way there in our little jeep, very much looking forward to enjoying a roast-type Sunday lunch, pork scratchings and all. With such an out-of-place attitude, we were, not surprisingly, sorely disappointed. The suckling pig was there in the small marketplace, a host of old women lost up to their elbows in the entrails of the animal. As they nonchalantly chopped bits from limbs here and there, it looked as though the dining table also belonged to the butcher. With all this flesh the flies swarmed and the heat enhanced the not too pleasant aroma of meat rapidly going bad.

When cooked the meat was probably delicious, but our appetite was gone. Hopefully, the few recipes below will be more palatable and enjoyed in rather more welcoming surroundings. (Gianyar is reputed for its sarongs and textiles—perhaps we were just looking for the wrong thing!)

BABI KECAP
Spiced Pork Cooked in Soy Sauce

It might be thought that in Indonesia, a largely Muslim country, pork would not be a significant part of the cuisine. However, there are a host of other faiths practiced in this generally tolerant country, and pork is especially enjoyed in places such as Hindu-Buddhist Bali.

> *Approximately 4 tablespoons vegetable oil for frying*
> *4 shallots (or 1 small onion), finely chopped*
> *3 cloves garlic, crushed and chopped*
> *1 pound lean pork filet, chopped into 1-inch cubes*
> *4 tablespoons dark soy sauce*
> *2 teaspoons dark brown sugar*
> *1 teaspoon freshly grated nutmeg (or 1 teaspoon ground nutmeg)*
> *1 clove*
> *A dash of salt and freshly ground black pepper*
> *1 cup water*
> *4 scallions, chopped, to garnish*

Heat oil in wok and fry the shallots and garlic until transparent.

Over a medium heat add the pork and fry for approximately 5 minutes. Reduce the heat and add the soy sauce, sugar, nutmeg, clove, and salt, and pepper. Stir and cook for a further few minutes.

Add water to cover the pork and bring the mixture to a boil.

Reduce the heat again and simmer, uncovered for 40 to 50 minutes or until the pork is tender and the sauce is thick. Discard the clove and garnish with chopped scallions.

BABI ASAM PEDAS
Hot and Sour Pork

1 pound lean pork filet
1 teaspoon salt
½ cup malt vinegar
Approximately 5 tablespoons vegetable oil for frying

SPICE PASTE:
6 shallots (or 1 medium onion)
3 cloves garlic, crushed and chopped
3 candlenuts (or macadamia nuts or skinned almonds), crushed
1-inch piece ginger, crushed and chopped
3 fresh chilies (or 3 dried chilies or 2 teaspoons chili powder)
1 tablespoon dark brown sugar
1 medium-sized can bamboo shoots, drained
½ cup water
Salt and freshly ground black pepper to taste
2 tablespoons chopped coriander or parsley leaves, to garnish

Chop the meat into small pieces, place in a bowl and rub with the salt and 2 teaspoons of vinegar. Set aside in a cool place.

Grind ingredients for spice paste in mortar and pestle, or place in blender and mix until smooth.

Heat 4 tablespoons of the oil in a wok and fry the pork in batches for 4 minutes each. Remove and drain on paper towels.

In remaining oil fry the spice paste for a few minutes, stirring continuously. Add sugar and remaining vinegar.

Add pork, bamboo shoots, and water and bring to a boil. Reduce heat and allow to simmer for a few minutes. Adjust seasoning with salt and pepper.

Stir for a few minutes longer and then serve and garnish with the chopped coriander or parsley leaves.

Serves 4.

SATAY

Kebabs with various marinades

In the recipe for Chicken Kebabs (*Satay Ayam*) in the Poultry and Eggs section (page 69), peanut sauce, which is very popular in Indonesia, is suggested.

Any meat can, however, be used in a satay. The marinades and sauces are very often peanut-based, but this isn't a hard-and-fast rule. In the following recipe either beef, lamb, pork, chicken, or shrimp can be used, and the peanut sauce (as given for *Gado Gado* on page 55) is excellent. A few alternative marinades are suggested below.

> *1 pound filet beef, lean lamb, lean pork, chicken, or 2 cups shrimp (heads removed, de-veined and cleaned, peeled but with tails left intact)*

Choose from below and make a marinade and sauce.

Chop the meat into ½-inch cubes and place in marinade. Leave for at least 1 hour in a cool place.

Thread the meat onto skewers (preferably bamboo, soaked for an hour before use). Barbecue the *satay* over very hot charcoals or under a very hot broiler, frequently basting with the marinade.

Cook until the satay is well browned and tender. Serve on skewers with sauce poured over them or leave *satay* uncovered and serve sauce in small separate dishes.

SERVES 4.

Marinades

BUMBU ASAM MANIS

Sweet and Sour Marinade

> *4 shallots (or 1 small onion), finely chopped*
>
> *2 cloves garlic, crushed and finely chopped*
>
> *4 tablespoons dark soy sauce*
>
> *1-inch piece fresh ginger, crushed and chopped (or 1 teaspoon ground ginger)*
>
> *½ teaspoon coriander seeds, crushed*
>
> *2-inch piece tamarind soaked for 10 minutes in 4 tablespoons hot water and then squeezed and discarded to leave a colored juice (or 2 tablespoons lime or lemon juice)*
>
> *2 teaspoons dark brown sugar*
>
> *A dash of salt and freshly ground pepper*

Combine all the ingredients and mix well.

SERVES 4.

BUMBU PEDAS
Chili Hot Marinade

6 shallots (or 1 medium onion), finely chopped

1-inch piece fresh ginger, crushed and chopped (or 2 teaspoons ground ginger)

3 fresh red chilies (or 3 dried chilies or 2 teaspoons chili powder)

2-inch piece tamarind soaked for 10 minutes in 4 tablespoons hot water and then squeezed
   and discarded to leave a colored juice (or 2 tablespoons lime or lemon juice)

3 tablespoons dark soy sauce

1 teaspoon salt

1 tablespoon vegetable oil

Grind ingredients in mortar and pestle, or place in blender and mix until smooth.

SERVES 4.

BUMBU KECAP
Soy Sauce Marinade

4 shallots (or 1 small onion), finely chopped

4 tablespoons dark soy sauce

2 tablespoons lime (or lemon) juice

2 teaspoons dark brown sugar

A dash of salt and freshly ground black pepper

Combine all ingredients and stir well.

SERVES 4.

TAHU DAN TEMPE

TOFU AND TEMPEH

Tofu (or *Tahu* as it is known in Indonesia) and tempeh are both products of the versatile soy bean. They are produced by processes which break down their indigestibility, resulting in highly nutritious and easily assimilated foods.

Tofu is a soft cake which has been prepared from ground soy beans and then pressed into white slabs; often for cooking it is cut up into cubes. Tofu is a Chinese invention but is considered daily fare in Indonesia. It is now widely available fresh, but will only keep refrigerated for up to three days, and should be kept immersed in water in a sealed container.

Just as the Chinese are recognized for their genius in creating tofu, the Indonesians, specifically the Javanese, are known for their invention of tempeh. Its production probably began at the beginning of the soy bean trade with China as long ago as 1000 C.E.

Tempeh is growing in popularity in the West, where it is sold in whole foods produce markets and health food stores in the U.S. It is usually bought refrigerated or frozen. It has always been popular in Holland. Tempeh is synonymous with Javanese culinary tradition and is used in hundreds of Indonesian dishes. Despite its relatively unknown status in the West, there would be a big void if it were omitted from any Indonesian cookbook.

The method of tempeh production is passed down from generation to generation and is very much a village effort. It is basically made of cooked soy beans which have been fermented by an edible fungus. The product varies from village to village;

the most prized tempeh is apparently to be found in Eastern Java. It is a very attractive food and looks like a slab of white crusted cheese filled with nuts. It has a very pleasant mushroom-like aroma and a slightly nutty taste. In Indonesia, the slabs are left to ferment in banana leaves and sold that way, but plastic bags are used in its production elsewhere.

Tempeh is extremely cheap in Indonesia and is packed with an exhaustive list of nutritious properties. It is very rich in protein, essential minerals, vitamins, and carbohydrates, but contains no cholesterol or saturated fats. Perhaps one of the first instances of Westerners being aware of tempeh was during the Second World War, when prisoners of the Japanese on Java were fed this strange food, which must have been a life-saver for many.

TAHU GORENG

Fried Tofu

Enough vegetable oil to deep-fry the tofu in a wok
Approximately ½ cups tofu cut into bite-sized cubes
3 tablespoons dark soy sauce
Chopped coriander, or parsley leaves, or scallions, to garnish

Heat oil in a wok and deep-fry the tofu cubes until crispy and golden brown. Remove and drain on paper towels, and place on serving dish.

Pour the soy sauce over the cubes, garnish, and serve.

SERVES 4.

TAHU ASEH

Tofu in Coconut Sauce

¼ cups tofu
Enough vegetable oil to deep-fry the tofu plus 1 tablespoon
2 Kaffir lime leaves (or 1 bay leaf)
6 large green chilies, chopped (or 6 dried chilies, or 4 teaspoons chili powder)
¼ cup dried shrimp, washed and soaked (optional)
2 cups coconut milk (see Special Ingredients section)

6 shallots (or 1 medium onion), roughly chopped

3 cloves garlic

6 candlenuts (or macadamia nuts or skinned almonds), crushed

A dash of salt and freshly ground pepper

A dash of sugar

Cut the tofu into bite-sized pieces and fry in the oil until crispy and golden brown. Drain.

Grind the ingredients for the spice paste in a mortar and pestle, or place in blender and mix until smooth. Fry the spice paste in the remaining 1 tablespoon of oil until fragrant, and then add the Kaffir lime leaves, chilies, and shrimp.

Add the tofu and the coconut milk and bring the mixture to a boil. Simmer until the oil separates from the mixture and can be skimmed. Discard the Kaffir lime leaves before serving.

SERVES 4.

TAHU GORENG KECAP
Fried Tofu in Soy Sauce

Enough vegetable oil to deep-fry the tofu in a wok

½ cups tofu cut into bite-sized pieces

6 shallots (or 1 medium onion), finely chopped

3 green chilies, chopped (or 3 dried chilies, or 2 teaspoons chili powder)

3 cloves garlic, crushed and chopped

4 tablespoons dark soy sauce

2 tablespoons lime (or lemon) juice

4 scallions, chopped, to garnish

Heat the oil in a wok and fry the tofu until crispy and golden brown. Remove and drain on paper towels and keep warm.

Grind shallots, chilies, and garlic in mortar and pestle and then add the soy sauce and lime juice, or place all ingredients into a blender and mix until fairly smooth.

Place the mixture into a small pan and bring to a gentle boil.

Pour the sauce over the tempeh and garnish with the scallions.

SERVES 4.

TAHU ISI
Savory-stuffed Tofu

Approximately ½ cups tofu cut into 4 large pieces

¼ pound minced beef filet

½ cup shrimp, cleaned, heads removed, peeled and minced

4 cloves garlic, crushed finely

1 teaspoon ground black pepper

A dash of salt

3 eggs, beaten

Enough vegetable oil to deep-fry the tofu

Halve each square of tofu.

Combine the beef, shrimp, garlic, pepper, and salt.

Beat the eggs and add to the mixture.

Stuff the mixture into the pieces of tofu and deep-fry until crispy and golden-brown.

Serve with an accompaniment such as a peanut sauce (page 55).

Note: An interesting variation would be to stuff the tofu with tempeh rather than the beef and shrimp mixture.

SERVES 4.

SAMBAL GORENG KERING TEMPE
Spicy Crisp-fried Tempeh

Tempeh is sold in *warungs* on every street corner. Everybody loves it, and expatriates have discovered what an excellent snack it makes eaten with spicy green chilies. Offices send out messengers to buy a big plateful at a very low cost. The following two recipes are probably the most popular snack-type dishes available.

1½ cups tempeh

Enough vegetable oil to deep-fry the tempeh, plus 1 tablespoon for spice paste

2-inch piece tamarind soaked for 10 minutes in 4 tablespoons hot water and then squeezed
and discarded to leave a colored juice (or 2 tablespoons lime or lemon juice)

A dash of salt and freshly ground pepper

1 tablespoon white sugar

2 tablespoons dark brown sugar

6 red chilies, seeds discarded, sliced diagonally and fried

6 shallots (or 1 medium onion), chopped finely and fried

SPICE PASTE:

5 cloves garlic, roughly chopped

1-inch piece fresh ginger, crushed and roughly chopped

Cube the tempeh into ½-inch squares and deep-fry until golden brown and crispy. Drain on paper towels and set aside.

Grind ingredients for spice paste in mortar and pestle, or place in blender and mix until smooth.

Fry the spice paste in the tablespoon of oil until fragrant.

Add the tamarind juice, salt, and pepper, and sugars. Continue cooking until the sauce thickens.

Add the tempeh, chilies, and fried shallots. Stir until everything is well blended. Remove and serve.

SERVES 4.

KERIPIK TEMPE
Crisp-fried Tempeh

1½ cups tempeh

SPICE PASTE:

4 candlenuts (or macadamia nuts or skinned almonds), crushed

1 clove garlic, crushed

1 teaspoon coriander seeds, crushed

½ cup water

½ cup rice flour (or strong white flour), mixed with 1 tablespoon corn starch

Enough vegetable oil to deep-fry the tempeh

Slice the tempeh into thin, ⅛-inch slices and set aside.

Grind the ingredients for the spice paste in a mortar and pestle, or place in blender and mix until smooth.

Add the water to the paste and then the rice flour and corn starch. Mix well.

Heat the oil in a wok. Dip the tempeh into the spicy batter and deep-fry until golden brown and very crispy. Remove and drain on paper towels and sprinkle with a little salt. Serve with tiny red and green chilies.

SERVES 4.

TEMPE JAWA
Javanese Tempeh

This is a local dish from Central Java.

1¼ cups tempeh
½ teaspoon salt
Approximately 6 tablespoons vegetable oil for frying
3 fresh red chilies, finely sliced (or 3 dried chilies, or 3 teaspoons chili powder)
2 fresh green chilies, finely sliced
2 Kaffir lime leaves
2 cups coconut milk (see Special Ingredients section)
2 tablespoons chopped coriander, or parsley, leaves, to garnish

SPICE PASTE:
6 shallots (or 1 medium onion), chopped
4 cloves garlic, crushed
1-inch piece fresh ginger, bruised and roughly chopped
1 teaspoon ground turmeric
2 teaspoons coriander seeds, crushed

Cut tempeh into small squares. Sprinkle the squares with salt and allow to stand for 10 minutes.

Heat 5 tablespoons of the oil in a wok and fry squares until crispy and golden. Drain on paper towels.

Grind ingredients for spice paste in mortar and pestle, or place in blender and mix until fairly smooth.

Heat the remaining 1 tablespoon oil in a wok and fry the paste, chilies, and Kaffir lime leaves until mixture is fragrant. Add the fried tempeh and coconut milk and bring to a boil. Adjust seasoning with salt and pepper, and stir to prevent coconut milk from curdling. Simmer for a further 10 minutes or until the sauce thickens.

Garnish with the chopped coriander, or parsley leaves, and discard Kaffir lime leaves before serving.

SERVES 4.

ADUK-ADUK TEMPE
Stir-fried Tempeh and Shrimp in Coconut Sauce

Approximately 5 tablespoons vegetable oil for frying
5 red chilies, seeded and sliced into ½-inch lengths
5 green chilies, seeded and sliced into ½-inch lengths
6 shallots (or 1 medium onion), finely sliced
2 cloves garlic, finely sliced
Kaffir lime leaf (or 1 small bay leaf)
1-inch piece fresh ginger, crushed and finely chopped
1 cup shrimp, heads removed, peeled, de-veined and cleaned
1½ cups tempeh, sliced into 1-inch cubes
A dash of salt and freshly ground pepper
A dash of dark brown sugar
1¼ cups coconut milk (see Special Ingredients section)
2 tomatoes, thinly sliced
5 tablespoons dark soy sauce

Heat the oil in a wok and fry the red and green chilies, shallots, and garlic. Add the Kaffir lime leaf and the ginger. Stir-fry until mixture is fragrant.

Add the shrimp and cook until they turn pink. Add the tempeh, salt, pepper, and sugar. Add the coconut milk and bring to a boil, stirring continuously.

Add the tomatoes and the soy sauce. Continue cooking until the coconut milk has reduced. Discard the Kaffir lime leaf before serving.

SERVES 4.

TEMPE GURIH
Curried Tempeh

1½ cups tempeh, sliced into bite-sized squares
Approximately 6 tablespoons vegetable oil for frying, plus 1 tablespoon for spice paste

Approximately 2 cups coconut milk (see Special Ingredients section)

6 green chilies, seeds discarded and sliced into 1-inch lengths

SPICE PASTE:

5 red chilies, chopped (or 5 dried chilies, or 3 teaspoons chili powder)

6 shallots (or 1 large onion), roughly chopped

3 cloves garlic, crushed

1 teaspoon ground turmeric

1-inch piece fresh ginger, crushed

A dash of salt and freshly ground pepper

1 teaspoon dark brown sugar

Fry the tempeh for approximately 5 minutes.

Grind the ingredients for the spice paste in a mortar and pestle, or place in blender and mix until smooth.

Fry spice paste until fragrant and then add the coconut milk. Bring the mixture to a boil.

Add the chilies and the tempeh. Simmer until the sauce forms oil on the surface. Skim and serve.

SERVES 4.

BUAH, PUDING, DAN KUE
FRUITS, PUDDINGS, AND CAKES

As Indonesian food tends to be served all together rather than in courses, a meal would not traditionally be followed by a pudding. The Indonesians love sugar, however, and many in the *kampungs* believe that it makes them strong. Sweets are not eaten as a dessert, but rather as we would have a chocolate bar or a mid-morning snack.

Fruits are abundant and delicious and are most definitely worth a mention by themselves. Following is a description of just a few of the fruits to be enjoyed in Indonesia.

Durian

Durian is the most notorious fruit in Indonesia, surrounded by a wealth of myth and controversy. Indeed, it is even believed to possess aphrodisiac qualities; an old Indonesian aphorism says, "When the *durians* fall, the sarongs rise." As many people love it as hate it. Because of the fruit's pungent and persistent smell, it is banned by hotels and airlines.

The *durian* looks rather like a very large and spiked pale green grenade, which opens into a creamy and segmented interior. For those who loathe the fruit, the taste could perhaps be described as something resembling acrid boiled onions. The best time to eat *durian* is when the fruit matures a little more and the segments are creamy and custard-like; the fruit then tastes rather like an incredibly indulgent and slightly alcoholic dessert.

Jackfruit *(Nangka)*

This fruit has a similar but crunchier interior than the *durian.* It grows much larger in size and has an amorphous, ugly shape. Jackfruit is mid-green in color and covered in blunt spikes. Its taste and smell are not pervasive like the *durian,* and it is extremely popular. The yellow segments are most commonly sold on the streets in little plastic packets.

The ripe fruit can be eaten as a pudding, but the firm, young fruit has an excellent texture for use in savory dishes and provides the principal ingredient for *Gudeg.*

Sirasak

This fruit also has a similar segmented interior to the *durian* and jackfruit, except that it is white in color with black, flat seeds. It is relatively small compared to the jackfruit; a medium-sized *sirasak* is comparable to a honeydew melon.

The flavor is deliciously sweet, with a slight sharpness which makes it extremely refreshing. It is popular as a juice.

Mangosteen

This is an exquisite, small fruit native to Indonesia and Malaysia. It comes from an extremely slow-growing tree which does not bear fruit for approximately ten years. The *mangosteen* is about the size of a tennis ball with a leatherish outer skin in a beautiful deep shade of purple, with a tough little green stem at the top of the fruit.

The flesh breaks apart into white orange-like segments which are firm and deliciously sweet and refreshing.

Rambutan

The name comes from the Malay word *rambut,* meaning "hair." This egg-sized and egg-shaped reddish fruit is covered in hairy spikes. It is usually sold in bundles of about twenty to thirty.

The fruit is often compared to that of a lychee, with a translucent flesh, a chewy texture, and a sweet taste. The fruit has a woody seed at its center.

Starfruit *(Belimbing)*

This star-shaped, yellow-green fruit is a popular thirst quencher. It has a delicate texture and tastes rather like a pleasantly watery apple. It has a high vitamin C content and is full of minerals.

Papaya

This was originally introduced to South America by the Spaniards and then to Southeast Asia via the Philippines during their long colonization of that country.

The papaya is a large, quite elongated fruit. It is medium-sized, measuring about a foot in length, with a diameter of about five inches. The fruit is harvested when yellow begins to streak through its green skin.

The interior is crammed with a tube of small seeds, which have to be discarded before the fruit is eaten. The flesh is soft and deep pink in color and has a delicate, sometimes slightly bland flavor.

The fruit is exceptionally healthful, containing vitamins A and C. The leaves contain papain which can help to tenderize meat and the juice of the leaves has been used in past times to guard against malaria.

Snakefruit *(Salak)*

An unusual looking roundish-shaped fruit with a brown, snake-like skin. The interior is segmented into three or four pieces and the flesh is a white, slightly translucent color. Its texture is crunchy and dry. Each segment is wrapped around a large brown pip. The taste is quite sharp and crisp, but slightly dry.

Jeruk Bali

Jeruk means "citrus" in Indonesia, and these large soccer ball-shaped fruits are the best of the citrus fruits found here. Sometimes known as a *pomelo* in other countries such as Thailand, the fruit is segmented just like a very large grapefruit with flesh the color of a pink grapefruit, but with a slightly drier texture and flavor.

These are just a few of the most delicious fruits to be found in Indonesia. Of course there are hundreds of others, some requiring an acquired taste, such as the *Duku* and the various types of *Jambu,* and the tropical favorites such as mango and pineapple are also plentiful. This section would not be complete, however, without mentioning coconut and banana, both of which play an important role in Indonesian cuisine.

Coconut *(Kelapa)*

Probably our most immediate image of the coconut is that of the fruit growing on tall, tropical palm trees lining exotic beaches. This is, however, a rather incomplete image when the uses of the tree and its fruit are considered.

The trunk of the coconut palm is used in the production of furniture, and the hair of the fruit is used to make matting and rope. Coconut oil is widely used in industries such as soap and food manufacturing.

Coconut milk, or *santen,* made by squeezing the shredded flesh into water, is one of the ingredients which makes Indonesian cooking distinctive. When eaten as a fruit, it is only the young flesh, which is almost jellyish, and the water which are consumed. The Indonesians also popularly drink the juice straight from the fruit, *es kelapa muda* (iced young coconut).

Banana *(Pisang)*

In the West we really have no idea of the hundreds of varieties, differing shapes, sizes, and colors of bananas available in Southeast Asia. In Indonesia there are approximately forty different varieties; the *Pisang Raja* (King of Bananas) is the type most commonly used in fried dishes.

Every part of the banana tree is used. Even the luxuriously maroon-colored banana flower is edible, and the young unformed bananas, with their chevron yellow and red designs, turn any patch of land into an exotic garden. The banana leaf is as versatile in use as the coconut palm, and aesthetically pleasing as well. It is used in making shelter and bedding as well as for dining plates. It is also used as wrapping for bouquets of flowers and even as a most effective umbrella.

Puddings and Cake

Sometimes it would seem that certain small and remote parts of Indonesian society live off all things sweet and nice, like the Badui people, who partly subsist on making a living out of palm sugar and cloves. They inhabit a secluded area high up in the hills west of the town of Bogor. A great deal of mystery and respect hovers around these Sunda-speaking people. No one is quite sure why they originally retreated to such a remote location, but one of the most popular theories is that they probably represent the remnants of the aristocracy of the Sunda Kingdom who lived in the hills around Bogor. In order to retain their animist culture and resist the spreading influence and invasion of Islam, they were eventually driven further up into the hills sometime during the sixteenth century.

There are basically two parts of the tribe: the Inner Badui and the Outer Badui, all of whom inhabit an area consisting of about twenty small villages. All Badui people observe a very strict moral code of living (they must not kill, steal, commit adultery, drink alcohol, swear, touch money, etc.), but the Inner Badui keep themselves pure by having absolutely nothing to do with the outside world. Anything outside of their villages that they need is obtained through the help of the Outer Baduis, who are permitted to have dealings with the outside world. They distinguish between themselves in their dress: the Outer Badui wear black or dark blue turbans and sarongs, while the Inner Badui sport coarse plain white cotton, all hand-spun.

An outsider is privileged to be allowed to visit these handsome, dignified, and proud people. It is not difficult to believe that they are respected for having "powers of wisdom." The Outer Badui people have even reserved one of their houses for occasional visitors. But as the journey to the Badui is difficult and arduous, few ever attempt to go there and so, for the time being, the Baduis remain safe in their mountain retreat.

Their villages are spotlessly clean and neatly arranged. It is fascinating to watch the palm sugar bubble away in ancient cauldron-like wells in little huts. From there it is elegantly packed into oval-shaped receptacles made out of palm leaves. The smell of drying cloves is fragrant and ubiquitous.

PISANG GORENG
Banana Fritters

This dish is extremely popular in Indonesia and is most commonly sold in the *warungs.* It can be eaten as a snack, a pudding, or an accompaniment to savory dishes. There are a number of different ways of cooking the bananas (and with or without a batter coating), but the following is probably the most popular way in which the fritters are served.

> *4 medium-sized bananas, ripe but still very firm*
> *½ cup white flour*
> *A dash of salt*
> *Approximately 1 cup water*
> *1 egg*
> *Enough vegetable oil to deep-fry the fritters*
> *Icing sugar, cinnamon, and nutmeg to taste*
> *Honey, golden syrup, or light cream to pour, if desired*

Peel the bananas and slice into halves.

Beat the flour, salt, water, and egg together to form a smooth batter.

Heat the oil until very hot. Dip the bananas into the batter and then deep-fry until golden brown.

Dust with the icing sugar, ground cinnamon, and grated nutmeg, and serve with the honey, golden syrup, or just light cream.

SERVES 4.

PANCAKE PISANG
Banana Pancakes

2 eggs, beaten
A dash of salt
½ cup white flour
Approximately ¼ cups coconut milk (see Special Ingredients section)
3 medium-sized bananas, peeled and mashed
Approximately 3 tablespoons butter for frying
Lemon juice, cinnamon, and honey to taste

Make the batter by beating the eggs and salt together and then whisk in the flour and coconut milk.

Mix in the bananas and beat until relatively smooth.

Heat a very little oil in a frying pan and then pour in a little of the batter. Swirl it around to coat the bottom of the pan and then cook until the pancake is lightly browned on the underside.

Repeat the process for the other side and then serve the pancakes in a pile, sprinkled with the lemon juice and cinnamon and accompanied by the honey.

SERVES 4.

DADAR ENTEN
Pancakes with Coconut and Sugar

¼ cups white flour
A dash of salt
2 eggs

Approximately ½ cups water
A little butter for frying

STUFFING:
Approximately ¾ cup freshly grated coconut flesh (or dried coconut)
¾ cup palm or soft brown sugar
Approximately ¾ cup water
Icing sugar, cinnamon, and light cream to serve

Sift the flour and salt into a bowl. Make a well in the center and break in the eggs, one at a time. Add enough water to make a smooth batter and beat well.

Heat a skillet pan and brush with butter. Pour in a ladleful of the batter and swirl the mixture until it covers the bottom of the pan. Repeat the process for the other side of the pancake.

Pile the pancakes when made and put to one side.

Mix the grated coconut, palm sugar, and water together and then cook, stirring continuously, until the liquid has evaporated.

Take approximately 1 tablespoon of stuffing and place in the center of a pancake. Fold over and tuck in the ends. Sprinkle with icing sugar, and cinnamon, and serve with light cream.

SERVES 4.

RUJAK

Indonesian Spicy Fruit Salad

This is eaten as a savory accompaniment as well as a pudding, and makes a really interesting variation to the traditional fruit salad by comprising both fruits and vegetables. Below, fruits and vegetables are suggested, but of course any combination of your choice can be used.

1 small pineapple, peeled and cubed (or 1 medium-sized can pineapple chunks)
2 bananas, peeled and chopped
3 crunchy green apples, peeled and chopped
1 small cucumber, peeled and sliced

DRESSING:
1 fresh red chili, finely chopped (or dried chili or teaspoon chili powder)

1 tablespoon dark soy sauce
½ cup dark brown sugar
2 tablespoons lime (or lemon) juice

Place all fruits and vegetables into a bowl and mix thoroughly.

Grind chili and mix with other dressing ingredients. Pour the dressing over the fruits and vegetables. Chill before serving.

WAFEL
Indonesian Waffles

Variously colored sweetmeats are very popular *warung* fare, and these types of cookies and cakes are sold all over Indonesia.

FOR THE SPONGE:
1 tablespoon dried yeast
Approximately ¾ cups lukewarm water
¾ cup white flour

FOR THE WAFFLES:
1¼ cups white flour
6 eggs
1½ cups caster sugar
Approximately 2 cups coconut milk (see Special Ingredients section)
1 tablespoon melted butter
½ teaspoon vanilla granules

Mix the yeast into the lukewarm water. Add the flour and mix until smooth. Allow the mixture to stand for about half an hour or until the surface becomes frothy and the volume has increased. Add the flour and knead with hands.

Beat the eggs with the sugar until pale. Pour the egg mixture, the coconut milk, the melted butter, and the vanilla granules into a bowl with the dough and blend until smooth. Allow the dough to stand in a warm place for approximately 3 hours, or until it has doubled in size.

Preheat the oven to 425°F. Heat a large enclosable mold pan, or approximately 15 little molds, and brush with butter. Fill mold(s) with some of the mixture and cover.

Bake for approximately 35 minutes.

SERVES 4.

LAPIS LEGIT
Fragrant Two-Tone Layered Cake

Some Indonesian cakes are incredibly light and delicate and make excellent accompaniments to afternoon tea or coffee. The following, along with *Kue Lapis* (a steamed and colored cake), is one of the most popular and elegant of cakes. The procedure is rather elaborate (the cake should consist of at least a dozen layers), but worthwhile.

> *1 pound butter or margarine*
> *A dash of vanilla essence or a few vanilla granules*
> *1 cup caster sugar*
> *7 medium-sized egg yolks*
> *Approximately 3 tablespoons light cream*
> *¾ cup white flour*
> *A dash of salt*
> *9 egg whites, stiffly beaten*
> *2 teaspoons freshly grated nutmeg (or 2 teaspoons ground nutmeg)*
> *5 teaspoons ground cinnamon*
> *1 teaspoon ground cloves*
> *3 tablespoons melted butter*

Beat the butter, vanilla essence, and half of the sugar until light and creamy.

Beat the egg yolks with the remaining sugar in the same way in a separate bowl. Mix the two bowls together and add the light cream. Carefully fold in the sifted flour and salt, and add the stiffly beaten egg whites. Halve this mixture into two bowls, and into one of them stir in the nutmeg, cinnamon, and cloves so that it now becomes brown in color whilst the other one remains plain.

Grease and line an 8-inch cake tin with removable base. Heat the broiler. Heat the oven to 300 to 325° F.

Pour a thin layer of the plain mixture over the base of the tin until covered and cook in the oven for a few minutes until just set, and then place under the broiler for a few seconds. Then brush with the melted butter to keep the cake moist.

Repeat this procedure, alternating colors, until the two mixtures have been used up.

Cook the finished layered cake in the oven for approximately 5 to 10 minutes.

Cool and remove the cake from the tin.

SERVES 4.

GLOSSARY

Acar (Pickles)
Acar Buah Sayur (Mixed Vegetable Pickle)
Acar Kacang (Peanut Pickle)
Acar Ketimun (Cucumber Pickle)
Aduk-aduk Tempe (Stir-fried Tempeh and Shrimp in a Coconut Sauce)
Arem-arem (Savory Rolls of Stuffed Rice)
Asam (Tamarind)
Asinan (Fruit and Vegetable Salad with a Sharp Dressing)
Ayam (Chicken)
Ayam Goreng (Fried Chicken)
Ayam Gurih Jawa (Javanese Curried Chicken)
Ayam Gulung Dadar (Chicken Rolls)
Ayam Masak Santen (Chicken Cooked in Coconut Milk)

Babi (Pork)
Babi Asam Pedas (Hot and Sour Pork)
Babi Kecap (Spiced Pork Cooked in Soy Sauce)
Bakmi Goreng (Fried Noodles)
Bakwan (Shrimp and Bean Sprout Fritters)
Bawang (Onion)
Bebek (Duck)
Bebek Bungkus (Duck in a Parcel)
Bebek Panggang (Broiled Duck)
Belimbing (Starfruit)
Buah (Fruits)
Bumbu Asam Manis (Sweet and Sour Marinade)
Bumbu Kecap (Soy Sauce Marinade)
Bumbu Pedas (Chili Hot Marinade)

Cabe (Chili)
Cabe Isi (Stuffed Hot Peppers)
Cap Cai (Stir-fried Mixed Vegetables)
Cengkeh (Cloves)

Dadar Enten (Pancakes with Coconut and Sugar)
Daging (Meat)
Daun jeruk perut (Kaffir Lime Leaf)
Dendeng Ragi (Sliced Beef with Coconut)
Durian (Pale Green Fruit)

Ebi (Small-dried Shrimp)
Empal (Spicy-fried Slices of Beef)

Gado Gado (Vegetable Salad with a Spicy Peanut Sauce)
Gudeg (Chicken and Jackfruit Casserole)
Gulai Ikan (Fish Curry)
Gulai Kambing (Spicy Lamb or Mutton Curry)
Gulai Udang (Shrimp Curry)
Gula Jawa (Palm Sugar)

Ikan (Fish)
Ikan Bumbu Pedas (Spiced Fish in a Hot Sauce)
Ikan Gurame di Goreng Kering (Crispy-fried Pomfret)
Ikan Kecap (Fish in Soy Sauce)
Ikan Panggang (Whole Broiled Sour and Spicy Fish)
Ikan Ujung Kulon (Fish Ujung Kulon)
Iringan (Accompaniments)

Jahe (Ginger)
Jamur Bungkus (Spiced-Steamed Mushrooms)
Jeruk (Lime)
Jeruk Bali (Large Citrus Fruit)
Jintan (Cumin)
Kacang (Peanuts)
Kacang Buncis dengan Udang (String Beans Stir-fried with Shrimp)
Kambing (Lamb)
Kambing Asam Pedas (Hot and Sour Lamb)
Kangkung (Stir-fried Greens)
Karedok (Raw Vegetable Salad with a Spicy Peanut Dressing)
Kecap Asin and *Kecap Manis* (Soy Sauce)
Kecap Manis (Sweet Ketchup)

Kelapa (Coconut)
Kemiri (Macadamia)
Keripik Tempeh (Crisp-fried Tempeh)
Ketoprak (Noodles with Salad and Tofu)
Ketumbar (Coriander)
Ketupat (Compressed Boiled Rice)
Kue (Cake)
Kunyit (Turmeric)

Lapis Legit (Fragrant Two-tone Layered Cake)
Langkuas (Galingale)
Lontong (Compressed Boiled Rice)
Lumpia Goreng (Stir-fried Vegetables Cooked in Pastry Wrappers)

Mangosteen (Small Purple Fruit)
Martabak (Beef-stuffed Savory Pancakes)
Mie (Noodles)
Mihun Instan (Instant Vermicelli)
Minyak kelapa (Coconut oil)

Nangka (Jackfruit)
Nasi (Rice)
Nasi Bumbu (Spicy Rice)
Nasi Goreng (Fried Rice)
Nasi Kuning (Yellow Rice)

Omelet Kepiting (Crab Omelettes)
Orak Arik Jagung Muda (Stewed Baby Corn)

Pala (Nutmeg)
Pancake Pisang (Banana Pancakes)
Papaya (Medium-sized, Fleshy Orange Fruit)
Pisang (Banana)
Pisang Goreng (Fried Bananas)
Peredel Daging (Meatballs in Coconut Milk)
Puding (Puddings)

Rambutan (Egg-sized Reddish Fruit)
Rendang Daging Sapi (Beef Rendang)
Rijstafel ("Ricetable"—distinctive Dutch-Indonesian cuisine)
Rujak (Indonesian Spicy Fruit Salad)

Salak (Snakefruit)
Sambal (Relishes)
Sambal Goreng Kering Tempe (Spicy Crisp-fried Tempeh)
Sambal Goreng Kol (Spicy Stir-fried Cabbage)
Sambal Goreng Udang (Fried Shrimp in Spicy Coconut Milk)
Sambal Kecap (Chili and Soy Sauce)
Sambal Terasi (Shrimp Paste Relish)
Sambal Tomat Cabe (Tomato Chili Sauce)
Sambal Ulek/Cobek (Crushed Chilies)
Santen (Coconut Milk)
Satay (Kebabs with Various Marinades)
Satay Ayam (Chicken Kebabs)
Sayur (Vegetables)
Sayur Asam (Sour Vegetable Soup)
Sayur Bayam (Spinach Soup)
Sayur dengan Santen (Vegetables in Coconut Milk)
Sayur dengan Telur (Vegetables Scrambled with Eggs)
Selada (Salad)
Sereh (Lemongrass)
Serundeng (Coconut with Peanuts)
Singgang Ayam (Baked Chicken)
Sirasak (White Sweet Fruit)
Sop Ikan Pedas (Spicy Hot Fish Soup)
Sop Udang (Shrimp Soup)
Soto Ayam (Chicken Soup)
Soto dengan Kepiting dan Asparagus (Crab and Asparagus Soup)

Tahu (Tofu)
Tahu Aseh (Tofu in Coconut Sauce)
Tahu Goreng Kecap (Fried Tofu in Soy Sauce)
Tahu Isi (Savory-stuffed Tofu)
Telur (Eggs)

Telur dengan Sambal Tomat Cabe (Hard-cooked Eggs with Chili Tomato Sauce)
Tempe (Fermented Soybean)
Tempe Jawa (Javanese Tempeh)
Tempe Gurih (Curried Tempeh)
Terasi (Fishpaste/Balachan)
Terung Goreng dengan Bawang dan Cabe (Fried Eggplant with Shallots and Chilies)
Tumis Tauge (Stir-fried Bean Sprouts with Tempeh)

Udang (Shrimp)
Udang Bakar (Whole Broiled Jumbo Shrimp)
Udang Goreng Asam Manis (Sweet and Sour Jumbo Shrimp)
Udang Goreng dengan Liquor (Fried Shrimp with Sherry)
Udang Masak Nanas (Shrimp Cooked with Pineapple)
Udang Rebus (Steamed Shrimp)
Urap (Vegetable Salad with a Coconut Dressing)

Wafel (Indonesian Waffles)

INDEX TO RECIPES

BIBLIOGRAPHY

Dalton, Bill. *Indonesia Handbook,* Fourth Edition.
Moon Publications, 1988.

Holzen, Heinz, and Lother Arsana.
The Food of Bali: Authentic Recipes from the Island of the Gods.
Hong Kong: Periplus Editions, Ltd., 1993.

Marahimin, Hian, and Roos Djalil.
Indonesian Dishes and Desserts. PT Gaya Favorit Press, 1990.

Jaffrey, Madhur. *Far Eastern Cookery.* BBC Books, 1989.

Owen, Sri. *Indonesian Food and Cookery.* Prospect Books, 1976.

Owen, Sri. *Indonesian and Thai Cookery.* Judy Piatkus, Ltd., 1988.

Scott, David, and Surya Winata. *Indonesian Cookery:*
Recipes from Java, Bali and Other Islands. Rider Books, 1984.

Skrobanek, Detlef, Suzanne Charle, and Gerald Gay.
The New Art of Indonesian Cooking. Times Editions, 1988.

Suyono, Roos, Christine Pangemanan, and Henny Tjakrawati.
Puspasari Jamuan Makan Indonesia. PT Jaya Favorit Press, 1991.